12-21-07

D1414244

Economics of Identity Theft

Economics of Identity Theft:
Avoidance, Causes and Possible Cures

L. Jean Camp

 Springer

L. Jean Camp
Indiana University
901 E. 10th St.
Bloomington, IN, USA
ljean@ljean.com

Library of Congress Control Number: 2007926498

Economics of Identity Theft by L. Jean Camp

ISBN-13: 978-0-387-34589-5   e-ISBN-13: 978-0-387-68614-1

Printed on acid-free paper.

9 8 7 6 5 4 3 2 1

springer.com

To my parents, who contributed significantly to this identity.

List of Figures & Tables

List of Contributors

Elaine Newton, RAND

Bennet Yee, Google

Barbara Fox, Microsoft

Allan Friedman, Harvard University

Ari Schwartz, Center for Democracy and Technology

Preface

Anyone who has ever bought a car, rented an apartment, had a job or conversation that they would rather not see in their employee review may find this book of interest.

There is a collision occurring in identity management. Identity technologies are problematic, and many see light at the end of the identity theft tunnel. Yet the innovation is driven by individual tendencies to seek convenience and business imperatives to minimize risk with maximized profit. The light is an oncoming identity train wreck of maximum individual exposure, social risk and minimal privacy.

The primary debate over identity technologies is happening on the issue of centralization. RealID is effectively a centralized standard with a slightly distributed back-end (e.g., fifty servers). RealID is a national ID card. Many mechanisms for federated identities, such as OpenID or the Liberty Alliance, imagine a network of identifiers shared on an as-needed or ad-hoc process. These systems accept the limits of human information processing, and thus use models that work on paper. Using models that work on paper results in systematic risk of identity theft in this information economy.

There are alternatives to erosions of privacy and increasing fraud. There is an ideal where individuals have multiple devices, including computers, smart cards, and cell phones. Smart cards are credit card devices that are cryptographically secure. This may be shared and misused, or secure and privacy enhancing. Yet such a system requires coordinated investment.

There are strong near term incentives for low-privacy, cheap and thus technically flawed identity systems. The expense is now, and the risk of fraud is in the future. The immediate loss of privacy becomes a systematic loss in security over time. Just as convenient credit cards have become even more convenient for criminals with the advent on e-commerce, the foreseeable diffusion of mobile commerce and pervasive computing will break many of the proposed Federated or centralized identity systems. There are better choices.

This book is organized with four major components, each more focused than the last.

The book begins with a discussion about how the digital networked environment is critically different from the world of paper, eyeballs and pens. Many of the actual effective identity protections are embedded behind the eyeballs, where the presumably passive observer is actually a fairly keen student of human behavior. Even a passive clerk notices when a two hundred and fifty pound man presents Emily Sue's credit card.

The second section takes the observations about the profound divide between ink and bits, and applies that to the immediate problem of identity theft. Identity theft best practices are included; but the core observation is that the average person can do nothing to avoid exposure to this risk.

The third section looks at defining the problem of security in the context of identity. What is the problem? That question is followed by a view at the proposed answers.

After the overview of the technology and proposals for identity management comes a series of possible futures. Examination of these futures indicates that there are two choices: surveillance, near term profits, and long term fraud versus near term expense, private secure credentials, and long term stability.

Acknowledgments

I would like to acknowledge my excellent doctoral students, first and foremost: Allan Friedman, Warigia Bowman, Camilo Viecco, Debin Liu, and post doctoral fellow Alex Tsow.

I would like to acknowledge all the participants of that early identity workshop, where the idea for this book was born. The two-day workshop included public servants, technologists, policy analysts, and civil libertarians. The early publication from that workshop provided the clearest set of definitions, and thus clear thinking, that I have yet to see on this issue.

Also, Dave Farber whose *ip* list provided pointers to many of the anecdotes included in this book.

I would like to acknowledge my spouse, Shaun McDermott, the one without who so much would be infeasible, including finishing any bit of work. I would like to acknowledge my children, who are the joy and light of my life, just because.

Finally, I would like to thank my colleagues at Indiana University School of Informatics. While there remains debate about how to define an Informaticist, we can only hope that any who fit the final definition are such fine colleagues and coworkers.

Table of Contents

1. Identity in Economics, and in Context

Unique identification today is much as it was when last names were adopted in Western Europe – all about money. Early on, governments adopted identity to enable taxation. Now businesses are creating and using identity systems in order to decrease their own risks, by shifting risks and fraud to the identified people. Companies seek profit in cheap credit, while individuals are burdened with the risk of ID fraud.

How much is it worth to have an identity, to know someone else's identity and to lose or protect your own? The technology is disguising these core debates.

Current investments in identity management are targeted at increasing the speed at which human-readable identity information can move through data and money processing systems. The result will be an even greater explosion in identity theft. There is another option: privacy-enhancing, hardware-based, fraud-preventing credentials. Yet the second option is expensive and threatens the income flow of data aggregators. Adopting the second option requires clarifying the profound confusion of identities, which work for humans, and credentials, which work for networked computers.

Identity is built and constructed within an economic context. Anyone who has ever left the office for the bar or the PTA meeting knows what it means to changes shoes and economic roles on the way. In each sphere we might introduce ourselves differently. Going from work to the bar indicates the transformation from productive employee to indulging consumer.

At some times and in some places, the identity "Professor" or "employee" is relevant. In others, it may be "author," "customer," or "parent". Each of these corresponds to economic roles. "Treasurer of the Parent Teacher Organization" indicates a trusted volunteer who will likely not leave a job worth many more times the ten thousand in the PTO treasury. Identities are specific or general, and defined by role and context. For example, consider the incredibly specific and simultaneously perfectly generic, "darling". This is defined entirely by context.

Even people with the most focused lives--those who identify themselves either through their paid employment or parenthood in public contexts-- have private interests within which they use different identities. Employees rarely pay mortgages through the office accounting system, and peace in marriage can be grounded on separate checking accounts.

Changing jobs results in a new identity in the modern sense of the word. A change in position may result in a different credit limit and different privileges on different networks. A change in jobs frequently means a new place to live, with an entirely new set of identifiers sharing soft magnetic charges in an old wallet. Park Street Video and the Science Museum memberships are discarded for Horizon Video and the Discovery Museum along with the disposal of the old employee ID. Some things will not change. Linking the steady essentials to the transient creates economic risks. I have always paid my credit card bills on time. Linking the resulting right to get a new card with a telephone number allows someone to use the transient to access the constant – by getting a cell phone and pretending to be me.

In terms of identity and authentication, a change in professional affiliation results in a change in authorization in some contexts but not in others. When can that be a problem? It can be difficult to fully understand the risks associated with keeping information linked or discarding it. The risks of keeping all the information around, and the risks of deleting information are both very real. Sorting all credit card numbers and associated PINs in a single computer file enables a quick recovery in the case of a lost wallet. Many self-help books about managing your finances recommend it. For example, Microsoft Money will help manage accounts. Yet the existence of this handy file increases the risk of loss, and makes possible a larger loss in the case of a copied file. Keeping no records of credit card numbers and not writing down PINs decreases the risk of wholesale loss, and are recommended computer security practices. This also increases the difficulty of recovery if there is a loss. In fact, since many users do not keep such records, credit card companies authenticate individuals on the basis of a Social Security number thereby opening one path to fraud (using a false SSN) to address a good security practice (unique PINs and codes that are never recorded). The risks are cumulative and sometimes quite subtle until the worst case casts ugly highlights on the costs.

Today identity is more than anything economic. And the technology used to create, utilize, and protect identities is increasingly ill matched to the economics and uses of identities. To understand the problems with constructing economically viable and useful identity systems, it is important to begin with an examination of identity papers. Because of the familiarity of the tactile traditional identity paper this model is often in mind when considering identity issues. Yet the paper model is flawed.

Where are Your Papers?

Identity papers are the technology that underlies the assumptions in many digital systems. Understanding the economically perverse system of modern identifiers requires taking apart the various functions and characteristics of identity papers. Then given these functions taking a look at the mismatches with digital technologies, the next chapter addresses the core symptom of a broken system: identity theft.

What is different about paper and digital identifiers? What do we want to keep about paper and what should we lose? What are the paper-based assumptions that can be embedded in identity systems?

Before the invention of the press, authoring was simple compared to copying. Things could get created, but only the rare document. An identifying document from the king was a rarity. Each letter was valuable. Only the most pain-staking copying enabled the survival of information from the Sumerians, through the Roman and Byzantine empires, through Arab universities and finally to Europe. To copy a document was in no way theft but rather the only way to save a manuscript. Mass production and widespread documentation approached the impossible. Without laborious copying any authored document would be lost. Each book copied consisted of a set of articles selected by the human copier. To copy was to edit, in that modern editing is the selection and ordering of material for inclusion. (e.g., Eisenstien 1979; Febvre & Martin, 2000).

Should somehow mass identity papers have been created; organizing records of them would have been similarly difficult. Even that most basic ordering – alphabetical order – was in no way standard before the printing press. As said by an innovator in the 16th century, "Amo comes before bibo because a is the first letter of the former and b is the first letter of the latter and a comes before b ....by the Grace of God working in me, I have devised this order." (Eisenstien, 1979).

Outlining paper and identity theft provides a good introduction to the most pressing issues. The challenge of identity and economics is a bit broader. To widen the lens, identity is considered as an analog to different kinds of problems. Is identity theft a plague upon a war or us? Each view presents a different kind of solution.

Identity theft is the misuse of private authenticating information to steal money. Protecting identity requires protecting privacy. Proving identity requires exposing information. The next two sections first define privacy as multi-dimensional, and then pull forward the economics of privacy.

The economics of privacy are not the economics of security. There are commonalities; for example, in both cases it is easy for merchants to make security and privacy claims, and hard for customers to verify the claims. Security and identity provides a classic free rider problem, as described in this section.

The formal discussion of economics of security ends the first major theme of the book: looking at identity in a new way. The second major theme is on how identity is broken online. The third primary discussion is on the technologies of identity. The final section doesn't offer comprehensive answers about a perfect identity system, because, by this point it is clear that there is no such thing, just as there is no perfect investment for all situations.

Identity being broken online underlies more problems than are immediately obvious. Not only are consumers and users unable to identify themselves, but also users are unable to identify merchants. Certainly in the history of alcohol abuse there may have been some person in a stall in Nigeria that believes himself to be in a bank. But the inability to distinguish a bank from a kiosk and a banker from a badly dressed fraudster indicate deeper flaws in identity than exposed by credit card theft. Identity ownership and flawed risk allocation underlie these problems. Spyware, bots, zombies and scams mean that not only can you not identify a merchant; you may be unable to identify your own actions. There are effectively three ways to prevent the kinds of fraudulent masquerades so popular on the Internet: third party assertions ("trust him"), first party assertions ("trust me") and social network judgments ("everybody trusts them"). The economics of these systems vary widely, and as a result these systems provide different kinds of economic signals.

The signaling is not working. There is a wide range of solutions. These include anonymous credentials; which are the technical equivalent of presenting yourself well without an introduction in a conversation. Although anonymous credentials sound fancy, they are extremely common and simple. Everything from dollar bills to theatre tickets are anonymous credentials. Identity-based signatures are another technology for identity, one that proves group membership. Identity-based signatures can prove email from Bob@microsoft.com is really from Bob at microsoft.com. The following chapter discusses that magic bullet – biometrics. Of course, placing biometric security in an economically broken system results in a broken biometric system. Finally, reputations are described. Reputations allow groups to form identities through rating various providers, as in the social network descriptions above.

Technologies create identities that are embedded into economics. Four vignettes that provide possible views of the future summarize all the possible paths: single national identifier, business as usual; ubiquitous identity theft; and anonymous identifiers. Each of these snapshots of possible futures highlights the potential promise and pitfalls for identity systems.

2. Modern Technological and Traditional Social Identities

Identity In a Community

Long ago there was one context that defined all. What you were and what you thought depended on where you sat: throne, bar stool, or the side of the field. Now, where you are sitting proves nothing.

Sitting at your computer you prepare to move some funds into bonds. Every year your retirement investing should become a little more conservative. So every year, the same week as your birthday, you reliably move 1% of your funds from the international equities market that has been so good to you, intro Treasury Bills. The return may be less, but it will also be less risky.

Opening the browser window you see the first sale. AOL/Time Warner is being sold. What? Who is selling it? This is not a managed account. You end up taking two minutes and going to Google to get your fund's 800 number, since all links to contact lead to email. While you listen to the hold music the accounts you have spend two decades building up are emptying. FINALLY A HUMAN ON THE PHONE.

"Stop!! Thief!!" you cry. "lock my account"

"Sir, if you could just verify your identity. What is your mother's birthday?"

4/16

"I am sorry but that is incorrect."

"SOMEONE ELSE CHANGED IT!! FREEZE THE ACCOUNT!"

"You will have to take this up with customer service. If a crime has been committed you must contact your local law enforcement. We can't do anything."

Not only is this imaginable, it has happened. A victim cannot prove himself the owner fast enough, even if she sees the account being looted. Identity systems are broken more fundamentally than at the technical level. Identity systems are broken, economically, and individuals are paying the price.

Yelling into the phone, watching retirement accounts descend slowly to nothing, how do you prove you are you? How do you connect all the work and hours you have put in with the wealth that suddenly seems so tenuously credited?

Long ago, lineage, location, and profession would have answered questions of rights and ownership. Choice of profession was a function of lineage and location. Potter, weaver, William's son, or the resident of the farm on the hill next to the manor could describe an individual with implicit and socially embedded information providing identity. But these names described the individual completely in one context because the context was small and the ability to track, confirm and share information was well within human abilities. Because the context was small, there were connections between everyone in the group. Such an environment today might be called a highly connected network or an information rich environment. Then it was simply the reality of a life that was likely to be short, difficult and extremely geographically constrained.

Indeed the adoption of these informal descriptions as last names was economic. The description weaver became the last name Weaver and William's son became Williamson because effective tax mechanisms required unique identification.

In that life, each name provided with it an evaluation of the person within the context of the community. Each description provided a reason to extend trust or not because each description provided a connection to this ubiquitous context, and to a reputation. Evidence of a 'good' family, wealth earned, a farm well tended, or a skill provided what would now be called information for a risk assessment and the potential to report any untrustworthy behavior to the community. Wealth was embodied in both tangible products and opportunity created from socially constructed identities. Today intangible production and wealth requires more carefully constructed identities.

Trust was based on identity, and identity was personal and family history. Such a history included an evaluation of behavior in past interactions and transactions. "An apple doesn't fall far from the tree." implies not that there were few distinct apples, but rather the larger tree defined each individual. It also meant no credit or quarter was given to the person identified as being part of a larger, distrusted family. As Snopes in the stories of Faulkner creatively illustrates, rising in the social and economic ranks was not made easier by association with a family that was not trusted as recently as the nineteenth century.

A person could improve his station in life to some small degree based on charisma, hard life, work, and luck using a positive local reputation. Apparently good weather and surviving a plague helped too. Individuals could not necessarily access even greater opportunities by escaping a bad reputation. Both traditional community suspicion of wandering souls, and modern mathematical models illustrate that the only reputation worth escaping is a bad one.

Today, the Western world emphasizes the worth and reputation of individuals and not families. Indeed, committing to a family is the most common path to bankruptcy, as the family with two working parents is at the greatest risk for bankruptcy. Children no longer necessarily enhance social stature. In the past, distinct identities were for strangers and emigrants, who entered without being integrated in the larger community. By contrast, today each of us is a package of identities in different contexts. Yet, these contexts are collapsing with digital networked information, and because of this resulting complexity the financial and personal risks are increasing.

Yet the brutal reality of risk is that proving you are you over the phone or on the Internet requires knowing only public information: date of birth, mother's birth date, Social Security Numbers. Individuals have lost control of identities – all the data publicly available about who we are. We are living the midst of a terrible collision – we use traditional public community information to confirm identities in a world of networked digital wealth. How did this come to be?

Papers vs. Avatars

In the paper-based environment transactional histories were sparse and accessible to few. Community networks and common recollection, with little documentation, held personal histories. Community mechanisms for physical spaces and communities break down for digital communities.

In the paper world, the physical person is inherently linked to the action. A transaction requires the presence of a body. Thus the body and the identity are linked. In particular this enables an enforcement system that depends in the extreme on bodily enforcement (such as imprisonment). Remote paper transactions required either self-verifying documents such as letter from a common friend, or a delay while paper documents were processed (e.g., a check being sent, cleared, then credited).

Increasingly, important transactions are entering the digital realm. Accordingly, trust depends on transactional history—credit records, educational history, employment history, and criminal or medical history (depending on the rules of the state). The extension of trust is based on records or transactional histories associated with some common identifier. Across administrative domains that identifier is often the Social Security Number (SSN). Within administrative domains the number may be an employer identifier or membership number. These numbers, including the ubiquitous SSN, are difficult to remember. These numbers are often pass phrases or record identifiers, built to function for the computer-. Neither pass phrases nor passwords are ideal for the individual who is being identified. The ability of humans to remember random information is quite limited unless the information is given some understandable framing. Thus digital identifiers often have some process for release for the person with whom the data are associated. Such a release of pass phrase or record identifier is most often based on information that can be easily remembered. Today a Social Security Number and a maternal family name prove worth for creditor, employer or, increasingly, authorization for the one-time purchase of discount goods from the web.

Computerization has made transactional histories detailed, and computer networks have made them available to many. The increased detail and availability of transactional history has made the value of the information on each specific transaction lower, while making the value of the entire compilation of data higher. Information about a specific transaction is easy to obtain, and thus less valuable. Yet the compilation of the information provides a detailed look into our daily lives, and thus the sum of information is more valuable.

The use of some small set of information to access a range of transactional records has two fundamental flaws. First, the correlation of information across different sources is the canonical privacy threat enabled by information and communications technologies. Second, the use of the same information in multiple arenas creates a security risk. That security risk is most clearly illustrated by *identity theft*. *Identity theft* is the misuse of information to masquerade as someone else to obtain resources or avoid risks.

The individual data that together form a 'proof' of identity are hard to locate or extract in a paper-based system. Consider the difficulty of locating a mother's maiden name and a Social Security Number for a stranger before networked digital information. Access to that information would require access to paper records, records that could be managed and secured. In a computerized and networked environment, such individual datum is difficult to conceal. Once the individual datum is located, the access data can be created by a simple combination. Then the person with whom the data are associated has been subject to identity theft. Note that identity theft is in no way associated with physical impersonation. Rather identity theft is the compilation of information in order to access the rights and privileges associated with that information. The inclusion of a name is necessary but not central to identity theft. The problem is experienced by the victim as the loss of personal information, not the loss of an internal sense of self. Yet the use of personally identifiable information to construct interactions in the market is so ubiquitous as to cause the loss of key personal data to be an assault upon identity as defined in the summary.

Compilations of personal and transactional data exacerbate the problem of using personal information for authentication. Conversely, the transactional data are valuable only in that they are correct. If the data are flawed (for example because of fraud or theft from loss of authenticating information) then the transactional data lose value.

Paper-based centuries-old concepts of identity are being imported into the digital age with unpredictable results. The same information - called identity - that links the achievement of a college degree, credit worth, health insurance risk, or a promotion is connected to emails and on-line purchase records at on-line merchants. The record of each web view can be traced to the login at a specific machine. Information entered into forms may remain on the machines in the users' profile or password manager. As the same identifiers are called to serve multiple functions with great variance in the value of the data, the diversity in resulting management practices increases. As these identifiers are linked to one identity, the threat to privacy and risk to data integrity increases. Trust is a significant issue in Internet use. For businesses seeking trust, the domain name has become an asset in building trust as well as an identifier. In systems where files or processors are shared, elaborate schemes have emerged to enable shared trust.

When a single set of data is used for multiple functions, this creates the problem of wildly varying management practices for the same data. Those who obtain low but nonzero value from identifying data obtain such data, and store it according to their own value calculations. In terms of identity and identifiers there is a tragedy of the commons.[1] Very high-value transactions and decisions—employment, professionals managing large transactions—use the same identity-specific data as very small transactions. Because the risk in low value transactions can be decreased using personally identifiable information at the most detailed level (e.g., social security numbers, universal identifiers, credit information) these managers keep data long term. Identifiers simplify price discrimination. Yet because the value of the transactional records is low the level of protection is low. Use of this data resembles use of the proverbial common—all parties have an incentive to use the data but only one has incentive to protect it according to the highest value. Any party seeking to subvert data will seek data or systems at the lowest level of protection and then use the data for authorization to subvert the security surrounding high value uses.

Many of the technical problems of anonymous transactions, linking identity to binary data, and access control have individually been solved. Yet adoption of the solutions has lagged. This is particularly problematic in e-government.[2] The services and purchases by government are significant, and the authority vested in enforcement and benefits agencies requires risk aversion in applications of policies.

---

[1] The tragedy of the commons occurs where there is some highly desirable shared resource that, if everyone uses it according to their own incentives, will be destroyed. The tragedy of the commons refers to the grazing commons, where it is in the interest of each farmer to add an additional sheep. However, if everyone adds sheep the commons will be over-grazed and destroyed. Similarly if everyone uses the same identifier, like a SSN, that identifier will be over-exposed, under-protected, and eventually made unreliable.

[2] Implementing the traditional paper-based functions of government using online interaction between governmental entities or between the government and citizens is e-government

Individuals, government and business suffer from the use of a single identifier for high value (e.g., Social Security benefits) and low value (right to museum discounts) transactions.

When the government uses an identifier the issues are more complex, because identity is far more problematic for governments. Governments both need to be able to identify their citizens, and need to be constrained from knowing their citizens too well. Often, the identity systems created for security results in being a handy way mechanism for undermining security by exploiting the trust in the system.

In the Battle of Algiers, the story of the Algerian struggle against their French opponents is told, in all bloody tragedy. Terrorist opponents of France they were, and also freedom fighters. The French instituted a policy of identification papers to determine who was trustworthy to move around the city. After a particularly ugly bombing, the Captain was shouting at the private for letting in the terrorist. The private replies, "Sir, his papers were perfect." The Captain angrily replied, "Only the terrorists have perfect papers." The average guy forgets his papers, or loses them, spills coffee on the picture, or forgets which paper goes with which authority. Passwords may not be subject to coffee spills but they are far easier to lose.

A single bit of paper embeds many things at once, by the very nature of paper. Consider a passport. A passport includes an identifier, the passport number. It lists some attributes, including nationality, sometimes height and weight. It includes personal identifiers, including date of birth and name. It includes a biometric[3] method of identification – a photograph. (Bowyer, 2004) Passports are used, therefore for both identification ("I am me") and identity authentication ("My government authenticates that I am me."). A passport links attribute authentication (citizenship) with identity authentication (name) to enable off-line identification (photograph and physical description data). All of these elements are combined in a single document, and that document must be shown in whole to provide authentication. This binding of attribute to identity for the purpose of authentication is made necessary by the power and limits of paper. A person cannot calculate the exponentials needed to make a public key system work – this requires computers. An individual cannot check if an attribute identified only by a number is valid in a highly dynamic system - this requires a network and highly available data.

In fact, passport errors are not terribly rare. My passport has been extended to July 6, 20011. However, I doubt I will be able to travel for the next eighty years on the same document much less the next eighteen

---

[3] A biometric is a physical , biological feature or attribute that can be measured. Examples of unique biometrics are fingerprints, iris patterns, and DNA sequences. Other biometrics are not unique and therefore not useful for authentication or identification, e.g., hair color, nose length, and height .

thousand. Typos and errors in documents are accepted because the tactile form of the document. It is unlikely a terrorist would ever tolerat an egregious typo.

The document holds up to scrutiny because, other than the typo, it holds together. It binds all the elements of what we think of as identity - identity, identifiers, and authentication. That collection of details inherently occurs with paper-based system but does not necessarily exist in digital systems. Assumptions about "document" which are really based on assumptions of "paper documents" can be misleading, and lead us into risk instead of security,

Clarity requires breaking the traditional paper system, the passport, the certification or the license, into its functional components and understanding the interaction of those components in a digital networked environment. Without that clarity, digital systems can be designed with vulnerabilities resulting from the fundamental concepts of identity and authentication embedded in technology. What are the parts of the passport or the national id? How can those parts be taken apart and put together so it works for the holder?

The Elements of Identity

An identity in an identity system is not about personality or style. An identity is a set of attributes corresponding to the appropriate identifier. An identifier distinguishes a distinct person, place or thing within a given context. A context of an identifier is often defined in the very name of the identifier – the student id number or the badge number defines where the identifier came from and where it is meaning. These contexts are called *namespaces* in digital systems and the difference between context and namespace is worth keeping. A context implies the larger world, the entire passport with the picture and the smell of the airport. A namespace is something smaller – just the number and the name and all the information inside the passport.

An automobile, account, and a person each have identifiers. The automobile has a license plate and the account has a number. The person may be associated with either an auto or account through additional information, e.g., serial number, or a certificate. One person, place or thing can have multiple identifiers. A car has a permanent VIN and temporary license plate. Each identifier is meaningful only in the namespace, and only when associated with the thing being identified. Therefore, each identifier can reasonably be thought of as having a <thing identified, identifier, namespace> set, e.g., <car, license plate, state motor vehicle database>.

In the human tradition an identifier has been a name, in a community. In this case the namespace is the community. Name space is literally the space in which the name is recognized. Identifiers can be strictly formal, with the case of an employee identification number. An identifier can be extremely causal, as with my brother –in – law, who is "Uncle Mud" in his immediate family, "Uncle Mike" in our extended family, and "Butter Boy" to a certain niece.

In an identity management system identity is that set of permanent or long-lived temporal attributes associated with an entity.

In a community identity is a set of attributes associated with a person in community memory.

It is this very significant difference that underlies the use of identity today, which often threatens security and privacy. Identity in a computer is an identity in an identity management system. Identity to the human is a set of memorable authenticating facts or attributes. People and computers are so fundamentally different that there must be very different mechanisms for identity in a community and in a digitally networked system.

Attribute

An attribute is a characteristic associated with an entity, such as an individual. Examples of persistent attributes include eye color, and date of birth. Examples of temporary attributes include address, employer, and organizational role. A Social Security Number is an example of a long-lived attribute in the American government system. Passport numbers are long-lived attributes. Some biometrics data are persistent, some change over time or can be changed, (e.g., fingerprints versus hair color).

The attribute of the employee id number mentioned above is employment at the issuing company. The attribute of Uncle Mud is that he was once immemorially in the doghouse. The attribute of Butter Boy is that he once spilled drawn butter thrice during a family visit to a seafood buffet.

"Uncle Mud" is a personal identifier only in a very small namespace -- that of one family. There are probably very many Uncle Muds in the many families given the many uncles in the world. The context defines *which* Uncle Mud and thus *who* is being identified.

Attributes are relationships or past actions. I am professor because of Indiana University. I am an account holder because of my bank. In my house I am Mama, simultaneously the most unique and common attribute on the planet.

Personal identifier

Personal identifiers are linked to exactly one person. Persistent identifiers consist with that set of identifiers associated with an individual human that are based on attributes that are difficult or impossible to alter. For example, human date of birth and genetic pattern are all personal identifiers. Notice that anyone can lie about his or her date of birth, but no one can change it. Personal identifiers are not inherently subject to authentication.

The employer identification number is a personal identifier. There are common employer numbers, especially low numbers as it is common in start-ups to start with the founder as employee number "1".

Mama is an attribute. It is also a unique and deeply personal identifier in the context of one family.

Identification

Identification is the association of a personal identifier with an individual presenting attributes, e.g., "You are John Doe." Examples include accepting the association between a physical person and claimed name; determining an association between a company and a financial record; or connecting a patient with a record of physical attributes. Identification occurs in the network based on both individual humans and devices. Identification requires an identifier (e.g., VIN, passport number).

Identification is the claim of a personal identifier. It occurs in some namespace by implication. For example, the Kennedy School of Government employs a photographer. She is an excellent photographer. Her name is Martha Stewart. She is no relation to the (detained) doyenne of décor, and no one ever accidentally calls Martha Stewart Inc for a photograph. Martha Stewart identifies a photographer at the Kennedy School of Government.

Authentication

Authentication is proof of an attribute. Identity as it is constructed in modern systems is an attribute, e.g., "Here is my proof of payment so please load the television onto my truck". Identity is often used where an attribute is being authenticated, e.g., "Here is proof of payment for television 1245678, please load television 1245678 in this truck." A name is an attribute and an identifier, but it usually is not used to provide authentication.

The employer identification number authenticates a current state of employment. The possession of the identification card authenticates the association of the employee and the employee identifier. The employer's database authenticates the employee identification number.

A common argument is that authentication is who you are; authorization is what you can do. This means that identity is an explicit mechanism to connect authentication and authorization. Removing identity, or making identity authentication distinct from attribute authentication, means removing the threat of identity theft. Identity theft is enabled because of the confusion between authenticating identity (I am Jean) and authenticating attribute (I am a good credit risk in this transaction).

Identity Authentication

Identity authentication of identity is proving an association between an entity and an identifier: the association of a person with a credit or educational record; the association of an automobile with a license plate; or a person with a bank account. Essentially this is verification of the <thing identified, thing> claim in a namespace. "You are John Doe." is identification while "Your documents illustrate that you are John Doe." is identity authentication.

Uncle Mud cannot be authenticated to an outsider. If I were attempting to present a fabrication, and his family cooperated, there is no way to prove that Uncle Mud was ever used for my brother in law. However, I cannot prove to you either that I am telling the truth without an extended process of legal swearing. So Uncle Mud is a personal identifier in a namespace but it is an identifier that cannot be authenticated.

Attribute Authentication

Authentication of an attribute is proving as association between an entity and an attribute; e.g., the association of a painting with a certificate of authenticity. In an identity system this is usually a two-step process: identity authentication followed by authentication of the association of the attribute and identifier. The automobile is identified by the license plate; but it is authenticated as legitimate by the database of cars that are not being sought for enforcement purposes. Of course, the license plate check may find an unflagged record in the database yet fail identity authentication if the license plate is visibly on the wrong car; e.g., a license plate issued to a VW bug on a Hummer. The person is identified by the drivers' license and the license simultaneously authenticates the right-to-drive attribute. Notice the difference between "Your documents illustrate that you are John Doe." (identity authentication) and "Your documents illustrate that you are a student registered at the University and have access rights in this building." (attribute authentication).

When Uncle Mud pulls out his credit card (which most assuredly does not bear that name) his physical possession of the card and the match between the signature on record and his signature confirm his right to use the card. That is an attribute authentication. The name is simply a claim. When the service provider also requires identification, ("May I please see your license?") then there is identity authentication that collaborates the attribute identification embodied in the physical credit card.

Authorization

Authorization is a decision to allow a particular action based on an identifier or attribute. Examples include the ability of a person to make claims on lines of credit; the right of an emergency vehicle to pass through a red light; or a certification of a radiation-hardened device to be attached to a satellite under construction.

After authentication, by credit card or a combination of credit card and personal id, then a charge is authenticated.

Anonym

(as in anonymous).

An anonym is an authenticated attribute that is not linked to an identifier. An identifier associated with no personal identifier, but only with a single-use attestation of an attribute is an anonym. An anonymous identifier identifies an attribute, once. An anonymous identifier used more than once becomes a pseudonym.

The most commonly used anonyms are the dollar and the euro. The most familiar anonyms are self-authenticating. The users authenticate the paper. The right to spend the paper is authenticated simply by the fact that it is presented. To hold a euro is to have an anonym that authenticates the right to spend that euro. These dollars, coins, euros, and shillings are anonymous tokens. In contrast, credit cards and debit cards authenticate an identity; use that identity to authenticate the attribute. The attribute in this case is the right to make charges. Credit cards are identity-based payment systems. Cash is token-based anonymous payment.

Pseudonym

A pseudonym is an identifier associated with attributes or set(s) of transactions, but with no permanent identifier.

Uncle Mud (who I cannot but hope does not read this book) is a pseudonym. It is one where there may be many instantiations (or incidences, or examples of general nickname of Uncle Mud).

Telephone cards are pseudonyms. Telephone cards or pre-paid phones use an authenticator multiple times in one context.

Identity options exist in more than money or telephone minutes. Disney World offers season tickets, where a season ticket holder can authenticate by hand geometry. Alternatively, Disney World offers traditional tickets. These are tickets where the ticket itself authenticates the right to enter the park – anonyms that verify the right to enter the park. Disney stores offer insured tickets, where the ticket is linked to the identity via payment mechanism. These tickets look like anonymous tickets. However, if the ticket is lost, the purchaser can go to the Disney store or office, cancel the previously purchased ticket, and obtain a new valid ticket by presenting proof of identity. Then anyone who tries to use the canceled ticket is flagged. This is an identity-linked ticket, where the identity of the user is explicitly not checked during use except for dispute resolution. All the family tickets to Disney were linked to my identity and my credit card, yet clearly they were purchased for use by my entire family. I could have also sent them as gifts to any other person who could have used them, but who could not have reported them stolen. The insured ticket has an identifier that is linked, by Disney, to the payment process but identity is not authenticated for use.

In contrast, passports explicitly reject the possibility of providing anonymity. A pseudonymous passport that simply identifies you as a citizen is not available. In the digital world, in theory, a passport could present a citizenship claim, then add a biometric to authenticate the citizenship/body claim and even enable a search of known criminals. In such a transaction the person remains anonymous assuming there is no match between the unique biometric and the list of those sought by law enforcement. The binding between the citizenship authentication and the person physically present is much stronger than in the case with the paper passport, yet the roles of identity claims are minimized.

Identity systems must be trustworthy to be useful. The more critical the context or namespace in which identities are authenticated, the more robust the attribute authentication must be. Making certain that no one is holding explosives requires stronger attribution than making certain that everyone seated in the plane purchased a ticket. Adding identity into attribute authentication can weaken an identity system by creating a possible attack because it adds an extra step. When identity is added to authentication attribution then the authentication becomes as strong as the <identity, thing identified> link. If the authentication has two steps (identity authentication, then <identity, attribute authentication>) this creates another opportunity to subvert the authentication by subverting the first step.

Direct attribute authentication ("Do you have a euro?") is more reliable than identity-based attribute authentication ("Do you have a euro credit?") in any case where it is easier to create a fraudulent identity than it is to create a false attribute. If dollars were easier to counterfeit than identities to steal, identity theft would arguably not be the fastest growing crime in the United States. If the process of arrest and enrollment in the American criminal justice system relied on personal attribute (i.e., fingerprint) first, before identity authentication (i.e., name and ID), then criminal identity theft would not be useful. Identity theft is worthy of its own discussion.

Modern identities consist of informal, social identities as well as sets of credentials. The credentials may be short-lived (a ticket to go to a theater), long-lived (date of birth), independent (right to see a Disney movie) or interdependent (right to see an R-rated movie).

Current practices combine the dependence in a dangerous manner. Many proposed identity systems take advantage of network information to share information and compile identities without recognizing the risks that criminals have exactly the same advantages.

The next step in this book is immediate information about identity theft, and possible practices to avoid them. Understanding identity theft will provide the groundwork for understanding the greater problems with and identity infrastructure.

3.   Identity Theft

The name of a thing is sometimes quite illustrative. The remote control offers the ability to implement preferences over a distance. A browser allows one to go lightly from one virtual space to another, browsing not committing to one thing as with the purchase of a paper. The transistor is characterized by changing, or transient, behavior in terms of electrical resistance. Goat's milk cheese is a name needing no explanation. Fireplaces are designed for fires, and compressors compress.

Yet identity theft is an odd moniker for a crime where, in the end, the victim is not required to pay for the items charged or stolen. Rarely are victims left bereft of their sense of self. Victims do not lose their memories, as in the science fiction version of the theme. People in their daily lives continue to forget, recognize, like, love, loath or hate them. They rarely lose jobs and even more rarely lose their lives.

The cases of fatal identity theft have been where stolen payment mechanisms have been used to purchase child pornography. Of the tens of people who committed suicide after a United Kingdom bust of 'child pornographers', based entirely on credit card purchases, only two killed themselves after being cleared. The guilt or innocence of the others is indeterminate. Most people; however, lose their credit scores, not their freedom or dignity.

"Identity theft" actually refers to misuse of Social Security Numbers by criminals to construct and utilize an alias that cascades through the financial systems. The trick is to obtain a correct name: Social Security Number match. The name: SSN match can be used to begin instant credit at any address.

After instantiation of a credit card it is possible to get utility service in the identity's new residence. Utility bills and a phone number can be used to provide proof of residence and obtain a state identity card, usually a driver's license.

Alternatively, the criminal could go to any of the thirty driver licenses authorities that have been found to have fraud. In particular, the entire New Jersey authority has been found to be rife with corruption. All the line employees were fired, and the name of the Bureau was changed. (CDT, 2003)

Begin with a Social Security Number move to cell phones, credit cards, and then all the other services that are based on "credit", funds extended on expectation of payment based on credit records, something very much like an old-fashioned good name. The phrase and the crime are an indicator of how deeply embedded the SSN is as authentication is today.

After obtaining a SSN and an associated address, the attacker obtains credit. Initially, the attacker pays only the minimum due. Such a practice provides the highest possible credit rating.

Identity theft is the major common individual risk because of identity-based systems. The efficacy of identity theft is based on the fragility of the SSN-based identity system. Social Security Numbers enable federated identity systems. Because of the federation of multiple identities, one authenticating element can be used to generate reams of credentials.

No one has one key for their entire lives – one that opens the car, the safety deposit box, the house, and the desk. Different keys are controlled by different entities. The bank issued the safety deposit box key; and an employer issues the key for the building. Yet each of these places shares one key in the digital databases when ownership information is stored – the Social Security Number.

A SSN is required to obtain and sign a mortgage, or for a credit check to rent. A SSN is required to open a bank account and obtain a safety deposit box. An SSN is required as identification to get a job. A SSN is officially not required to obtain phone service; however, phone companies often simply refuse by not responding to requests with other identification. Having one key shared by all these organizations for all the locks in a person's life is unwise in terms of security and risk management, a disaster waiting to happen. It is this consistent relentless practice in the information realm that has caused identity theft.

Who would design a system where one key fits every lock in a person's life, and that person is required to give copies of the key to everyone with whom they have any chance of sharing a lock? It is tempting to explain this away with some false wisdom, like the jokes about committees where "None of us is as stupid as all of us." But in fact it is something more fundamental than the tendency of bureaucracy to use what works until it fails catastrophically. The one-lock-fits-all is based in part of the agrarian concept of identity that is deeply embedded in our humanity; that is, the idea that we have a single meaningful social and human identity.

Most importantly, the design is a result of *failure to design*. One system worked. Reliance on that system resulted in a collective failure to effectively move authentication and identifiers into the information age. The credit agencies and data brokers that profit dominate the resulting policy debate.

Paper-based identity systems link attribute, identity, and authentication into a single stand-alone document. SSNs worked fairly well in a paper-based system. The availability of networked data opens entire new vistas of possible systems. However, it simultaneously destroys the assumptions on which paper-based systems are built. Networked data is undermining the assumptions of "secret" information on which paper systems depend. "Secret" information is not information that is in every database, from Amnesty International donation records to the Zoo Family Membership.

The risks created by this shift are not equally distributed. Organizations can utilize the value of databases without protecting them. The value to the organization is in having the data; not in preventing others from having what is essentially public data.

Identity theft victims for a very long time were quite left in the cold. However, now that identity theft is the fastest growing crime, victims have some company and some legal support. There is Federal legislation making identity theft a crime. Before that legislation it was sometimes difficult to obtain a police report, as needed in recovery for identity fraud.

The Identity Theft Assumption and Deterrence Act, (918 USC 1028) in addition to prohibiting the construction of fake identification documents regardless of their use, requires the Federal Trade Commission record these complaints. However, the FTC does not investigate the complaints, rather the FTC keeps a database of cases, uses this database for research and tracking of cases, and provides a listing of law enforcement agencies that investigate complaints. The complaint numbers from identity theft victims obtained under the law must be provided to Federal officials in order to track the problem as it expands. Currently the FTC has a database approaching a million identity theft cases.

The Fair and Accurate Credit Transaction Act of 2003 defined identity theft as "fraud, attempted or committed using identifying information without authority". The FACT enabled ID theft victims to place 'fraud alerts' on credit files, and thus decrease the risk of loss in the future. FACT also created a National Fraud Alert system.

The 2004 Act greatly increased penalties for identity theft, however, the practices that lead to identity theft (in particular the use of Social Security Numbers by businesses) have not been curtailed. Interestingly enough, the 2004 bill included particularly stringent punishments for using identity theft in conjunction with a terrorist attack. This explicit recognition of the use of identity in implement terror attacks is almost as explicitly ignored in anti-terror programs, as some proposals function only if identity theft were not possible.

State laws that cover identity theft also usually cover criminal identity theft. Yet some are too focused on identity theft as a financial act, rather than as a device to commit other crimes. For example, the Massachusetts law makes it criminal to obtain information in order to pose ("falsely represent oneself, directly or indirectly, as another person") as another person or to obtain financial gain or additional identity information.

Specific identity theft laws have been passed in the majority of states, more than forty. In the remaining states identity theft is covered under fraud statutes and prohibitions on providing false information in a police report. Yet no state has a comprehensive mechanism for recovering from criminal identity theft. Once a criminal assumes a trustworthy identity as an alias, that identity cannot be trusted.

Avoiding Identity Theft, Individually

The best investment in avoiding identity theft is not a shredder but a phone call. The best way to prevent identity theft is to limit dissemination of your credit information. Of course, credit reporting companies make money by selling information. It is therefore in the interest of credit reporting companies to distribute individual information as broadly as corporately possible. Providing false information does not harm credit card companies. The company's preference is more information, not less, and accuracy has historically been of little concern to the industry. In fact, credit reporting companies reported prurient gossip until the Fair Credit Reporting Act prohibited the practice. Therefore it is a good practice to confirm the state records marked as ones that have opted out, rather than counting on the company to maintain the status of the records.

Avoid Unwanted Offers

Opt-out of offers of credit. A credit offer in the mailbox allows an identity thief to easily begin a range of thefts. To opt out of pre-approved credit offers call the three major credit bureaus or use their mailing address. Following is the contact information.

> Equifax
>
> (888) 567-8688
>
> Equifax Options, P.O. Box 740123
>
> Atlanta GA 30374-0123.
>
> Experian (formerly TRW)
>
> (800) 353-0809 or (888) 5OPTOUT
>
> P.O. Box 919, Allen, TX 75013
>
> Trans Union
>
> call (800) 680-7293 or (888) 5OPTOUT
>
> P.O Box 97328, Jackson, MS 39238.

The sites that are at the top of the Google search, my-free-credit-report.com, will connect to sites that require signing up for an expensive credit-monitoring service. The only free credit reporting site is AnnualCreditReport.com.

Encouraging employees to make such a phone call is an excellent investment for managers. A person with a lost identity will have difficulty obtaining credit, traveling, and can even be prevented from traveling internationally. After identity theft it takes the average victim more than two thousand hours to recover. Thousand of hours or time will inevitably impinge on work as well as personal time.

To avoid other "offers" of questionable value, individuals can add their names to the Direct Marketing Association's Mail Preference Service. The Direct Marketing Association offers an on-line form at:

http://www.dmaconsumers.org/offmailinglist.html

Of course, given the interest in the DMA in maintaining lists that are as large as possible, the form may move around the site.

The Federal government has provided a Do Not Call list, based on the failure of much-vaulted self-regulation in privacy. Information on the National Do Not Call list can be found at https://www.donotcall.gov/. Notice that charities are not prohibited from contacting numbers on the Do Not Call list; so all calls will not cease. Also, some companies with which you are doing business have a right to call individuals on the Do Not Call list.

Keep Your Information Close

In the case of banking transactions, lying about a Social Security Number is a crime. In the case of video stores, grocery preference cards, and many other applications the ethical case for lying about Social Security Numbers is solid only if you are certain that the Social Security Number is false. One way to do this is to select a prefix that is not geographically meaningful.

Unless you are paying for your medical services with Medicare or Medicaid, there is no law requiring that you provide your SSN to any medical provider.

Individuals can present a random Social Security Number when presented with an inflexible request from a place of business. Such an approach will reduce the individual risk of identity theft, and the value extracted from each person as a customer.

The following nine-digit numbers are analogous to Social Security Numbers:

Any field all zeroes
First digit "8"
First digits "73" – "79"

By choosing one of these numbers and using it consistently you can have a nine digit identifier that does not place you at risk for identity theft. Most organizations do not have a valid use for SSNs, and simply need an identifier. Particularly if the organization intends to give you an authenticating card with the number printed on it, having a false number lowers risk of identity theft.

No web site has any right to demand that you enter a Social Security Number. Request for a SSN should be a warning flag. Never enter your Social Security Number in a web site.

Some businesses will check your Social Security Number on line; so providing a false number is not feasible. In this case, explain that the SSN the company so covets is worthless, as the number has been used in identity theft. Explain that your counsel has recommended that it not be provided. Faced with determination, most companies will provide an alternative method for proving identity. Of course, these alternative methods will work far better to provide authentication of identity. These methods rarely provide the company with information that can be used to commit fraud. For example, a copy of a drivers' license on a fax will provide date of birth, address, certain disabilities (e.g., a need for glasses), and a drivers' license number. Since few organizations use such information without a SSN to authenticate, the information does not generate as much risk.

Some companies essentially force requirement for SSNs. Phone companies have particularly mastered this feat. A decade ago, providing a deposit was adequate to obtain phone service without a SSN. SBC Communications requires the customer, to fax a request for service with the penitent's passport number and drivers' license information.

Employers and providers of financial services need the Social Security Number of the individual to know their customers for money laundering, and to confirm taxation. No other organization, the phone company, the video rental store, the local charity – needs the information. Not sharing it is the best protection. Having an alternative nine-digit number will create a comfortable mechanism for dealing with intrusive demands for information.

Protect Your Postal Mail

It is not possible to prevent banks from printing full account numbers on banking statements, and some argue that it is desirable. It is possible to make certain that the mailings, ripe for identity theft, are not readily accessible. An old fashioned mail slot into the house is far preferable to a standard open suburban mailbox. These mailboxes are easy to use, and require a key to extract the larger documents. However, include in the cost the money for a tip for your postal carrier. The boxes are as easy to use for the recipient of the mail, but are not optimized for the carrier.

On the net, the Mailbox Guy offers mailboxes from traditional to deeply paranoid. $200 may seem a large investment for a mailbox, yet it is an order of magnitude cheaper than identity theft. The secure mailboxes also keep mail reliably dry

One form of harassment or technique for implementing identity theft is to put in a short term change of address form. If this attack is used, then the documents will simply be lost. Change of address forms were traditionally protected only by the law, not by process. For example, at Cambridge Savings Bank a change of address requires that the bank send a letter to the old address. The account holder must receive the letter, and then return the enclosed form with account information added. The account information is asked for on the form but not provided by the bank. Sending a message and requiring a reply is called *challenge and response* in computer security.

The postal system handles many more magnitudes of change orders than Cambridge Savings Bank. So the approach adopted by the Postal Service is to send a notification to the address from which mail is being directed. The person at the address will receive a change of address at the time the change of address is implemented. So while some mail will be lost, a victim will be notified.

In the event of a malicious change of address, the avenue of response runs to the local Postal Inspector. Postal Inspectors are the police of the United States Postal Office. As filing a false change of address form is a crime, they will both investigate concerns and endeavor to find for the responsible party. There is a listing of postal inspection offices at http://www.usps.com/ncsc/locators/, where it is easy to locate the nearest

The final way to protect mail is to buy a shredder. Use the shredder to prevent mailings with valuable information from going out in the trash.

Check Your Records

First, obtain your Personal Earnings and Benefit Estimate. Currently the Social Security Administration is required to *mail these documents*. Since the SSA is required to mail the documents, the SSA must purchase mailing lists. The best mailing lists have errors rates on the order of a tenth of a percent. The SSA must mail millions of reports, and with tens of millions of Americans tens of thousands of reports are mailed to incorrect addresses. The policy places every person at risk, as the error may be a simple as a transposed house number. The policy was a misconceived Congressional response to the authentication choices selected by the Social Security Administration when they decided to make the service electronically available. Mailing PEBES reports is an open invitation to commit identity theft. However, the Social Security Administration is required to issue these invitations to fraud by an act of Congress.

A second set of documents that would be of use is credit records. The numbers above provide relief from the flood of pre-approved credit offers. The numbers below provide a way to order credit records and therefore check their validity. There are also credit-monitoring services that notify their subscribers every time their credit is checked or an account is opened. Such a service is available but neither friendly not responsive, from the three major credit agencies at the numbers below. Be prepared to spend either time or money. Each agency has its own number:

Equifax: (800) 685-1111
Experian (formerly TRW): (888) EXPERIAN (397-3742)
Trans Union: (800) 916-8800

And, incidentally, no one from Nigeria will even offer you tens of millions of dollars over email. Speaking of Nigeria here is another suggestion.

Beware Of Express Checks From Distant Purchasers

An increasingly common scam both directly obtains cash from a victim and provides banking information for the scammer, when completely successful. This scam applies to those selling high value items over the web. A foreign national contacts Unlucky and purchases the product by check, often from a UK or Irish bank. Unlucky deposits the check, waits seven days and then sends the shipping amount by Western Union and the goods by freight. Unlucky has become engaged in money laundering, in addition to being subject to plain vanilla theft of goods.

This result could be easily addressed. Funds could be made available as soon as checks clear, and not before. Customers could be provided with two numbers: current funds and funds pending. The customer could then know when the pending funds are in fact available. Even if the customer queries the bank, the teller will not provide them with the status of all funds.

International checks often take two weeks to clear. Express clearing is one mechanism to address this type of fraud. Refusing to take payments over the amount of purchase is also reasonable. International checks can be created, fairly convincingly, on a high quality printer. Never send goods until the payment is cleared. Recently this fraud was expanded to sending checks to "winners" of "lotteries". The amount printed on fake certified check is immediately available for withdrawal as a courtesy as soon as it is deposited, or shortly thereafter. However, the bank may not know the fact that the check is false for ten days or more.

PayPal presents a similar risk. PayPal offers assurance that a payment has been received before the sender has lost the ability to recall the payment. Purchase of high value goods on PayPal therefore requires either withdrawal of funds by the recipient, or patience by the person who is paying.

Of course, to become a true criminal Unlucky need not sell high value goods over the Internet. He could simply have lost control of his Social Security Number.

Protect Your E-Mail

The best immediate action most users and companies can take to decrease their risk of dangerous information exposure is to change browsers and email programs. This is a common suggestion, and many dismiss it as intra-IT politics. After all, the explanation of anti-Americanism common in IT circles is that anti-American populists abroad feel about America how Silicon Valley feels about Microsoft; except America has tanks.

Yet this is not a case of professional lack of courtesy. The American Department of Homeland Security's US Computer Emergency Readiness Team recommended using any browser but Explorer in 2002 for security reasons. The code in Explorer is so deeply embedded into the operating system, for marketing reasons, that there have been vulnerabilities that literally cannot be fixed without an entire operating system update. The Department of Defense has a report on its own use of open source systems including browsers, and the National Security Agency distributed a version of Linux optimized for security, at no cost to download. Explorer and Outlook are so intertwined with the underlying operating system that securing the operating system from either is problematic.

This is not American government politics. The German Federal Office for Information Security (BSI) told the Berliner Zeitung in September of 2004 that Internet users should switch to Mozilla or Opera. The Federation of German Consumer Organizations (Vzbv), the rough German equivalent of the American Consumers Union, recommends that users have extra care if they choose to stick with Explorer. Vulnerabilities make it such that Explorer and Outlook, particularly when combined, have cost customers or Dresdner bank their bankbooks.

You Are Helpless

The essence of the manner and the core problem of digital identity is that there is nothing you can do. The above are useful best practices. There is no way for an individual to protect himself or herself from identity theft. It is the lack of interaction with the individual that

Birth announcements from newspapers are available on-line. This means that given a birth date and an ability to search the Internet, any person can find your mother's maiden name. Indeed, increasingly women do not change their names so that date of birth allows you to know mother's maiden name. When your parent dies, the survivors are listed. Every mother's obituary is a gold mine for identity thieves,

Social Security numbers must be given to rent a house or even a DVD. Employers, family members, and roommates have stolen identifying information and thus financial identities.

We can choose to live in a society without obituaries and without white pages. Or we can construct an identity system that forces financial institutions to invest in devices. Passwords, user ID's and secret questions are designed to save money for the vendors by placing risk on the individual.

As individuals and organizations, we can muddle forward into identity confusion or we can design a system that works by not being shared.

Identity versus Risk Management

If your identity is valuable to you, imagine how valuable it must be for a fugitive who could not only use your credit but also your right to freedom. A person engaged in some larger crime, or one more severely punished, can use a nice clean identity to save time and trouble during interactions with law enforcement. A clean identity can prevent a person wanted on one crime being held when stopped for another. A clean identity can result in a person committing a third violent felony from being held as a violent felon when stopped on a traffic ticket or arrested for a misdemeanor. A nice clean identity in the hands of a criminal becomes an alias, and the original person identified by the authenticators claimed by the identity becomes a victim of criminal identity theft.

"Criminal identity theft" as it occurs in the United States is a multi-stage process that requires the systematic organizational failure in the use of a readily available database of biometrics (in other words, fingerprints). To begin a criminal commits identity theft and obtains a drivers license. Then, when arrested, the criminal presents this false identification information. The data from the false authenticating documents are entered into the national fingerprint database under the claimed name. The fingerprints are not compared with those already in the database because the system is keyed on claims of identity (name and date of birth) rather than the persistent identity-authenticating attribute (fingerprint). Of course, the criminal never shows up for the trial having escaped the net by using another's good name.

A warrant is issued in the name of the criminal identity victim. Eventually the unlucky victim is stopped in traffic, or an officer arrives at the victim's house. The criminal identity theft victim discovers the theft only after being arrested for another person's crime. At that time Unlucky's fingerprints are compared to the criminal's. Then the criminal's fingerprints are compared with all other fingerprints in the national fingerprint database, often but not always yielding a match.

Compare the entering of names (identities) with the direct entering of fingerprints (biometric attributes). The entering of a name asks the question, "Is this claimed identity in the system?" The attribute authentication question, "Are the fingerprints of this body in the database of criminals?" offers a more reliable response.

Criminal identity theft illustrates that biometrics can deliver the wrong answer more quickly and with a greater degree of precision than paper-based identity systems. Biometrics are only as reliable as the process of enrollment.[4] If criminal's fingerprints are enrolled under the Unlucky's name, then the police will seek Unlucky when the warrant is issued.

Fingerprints are not validated against an arrested person's assertion of identity during the arrest procedure. This failure to verify identity allows high-risk multiple-offense felons to be classified as the low-risk single-arrest identities they present. The failure to verify every fingerprint against possible identity theft not only puts law enforcement personnel inappropriately processing dangerous multiple offenders at risk; this failure also increases the value of stolen identities of the innocent.

Fingerprints are not validated because fingerprint validation and the corresponding process predate computers. Having humans search fingerprint records is expensive, and time consuming. Having computers search fingerprint databases is cheap, but requires a change in processes that have become culture.

---

[4] Enrollment is the process of entering initial records with biometrics. A biometric is only useful if it is associated with attributes (e.g., criminal records). The creation of a biometrics: attribute record is enrollment.

One possible response to criminal identity theft is that every set of fingerprints is evaluated against a claimed identity then entered. Such a response would be far-sighted, rational, and embed an understanding of the value of biometrics as authenticating identifiers.

Instead the various Criminal Identity Acts create a set of identification papers that victims of identity theft can show to officers in the covered jurisdictions. The victim of criminal identity theft obtains a document that verifies that a criminal uses the person's identity as an alias, and the bearer is not the criminal. The bearer of this certificate can then present the certificate to law enforcement to attest to his or her innocence.

The initial dependence on the constructed identity rather than the biometric attribute allows an attack on the law enforcement system, allows wanted criminals to escape from police custody by whitewashing their criminal records with others' good names. This creates an arms race, whereby the criminal can now create forged documentation claiming to be the innocent party, or more simply generate yet another false identity to use in the next legal interaction. The problems of international travel for victims of criminal identity theft have not been solved.

Criminal identity theft and the legislative response to the problem illustrates much more than the failure of a process for enrolling criminals in the national database of fingerprints. It illustrates the misunderstanding of authentication, identity, identification and attributes. Tragically this misunderstanding is being widely applied in the effort to secure America against terror. In seeking to provide security, multiple identification mechanisms are being implemented. Yet many confuse identification with authentication, thus creating risk rather than enhancing security.

At the Federal level in the US, there is a Transportation Security Administration "no fly list" and also a Computer Assisted Passenger Screening System (CAPSS) list. Without addressing the widely cited possibility that the no-fly list is used to limit efficacy of political opponents of the Bush Administration (Lindorff, 2003; LA Times, 2004) CAPSS can be addressed in terms of its efficacy in its stated goal. A similar list, the Computer-Assisted Passenger Pre-Screening System (CAPPS II), is being developed by the TSA and Homeland Security. Notice that no system is perfect and in every system there will be failures, even in theory (Aslam, Krsul, & Spafford, 1996; Landwehr, Bull, McDermott & Choi, 1994).

CAPPS II and CAPSS systems embody the perfect failures of static lists of identities. Static lists provide identifiers associated with people who have proven to be untrustworthy in the past, or who are expected to be untrustworthy in the future.

With a static list of identities, an individual is either on or off the list. It is not too hard to find out if you are on the list. Being on the list can be seen as a rating. A serious attack requires first avoiding security scrutiny. To implement the attack, the first round is to determine if the identity used for the attack is one that will result in scrutiny. Therefore, the obvious first effort is to determine a set of identities that will certainly not result in being subject to scrutiny. The less random the scrutiny, the easier it is to avoid.

Currently the no fly and security checklists are static. (Chakrabarti & Strauss, 2002) In addition, there are well-known factors that determine security scrutiny. Buying one-way tickets and having no frequent flyer number result in certain scrutiny. Having a frequent flyer number, buying a round trip ticket, and flying coach result in no scrutiny. These well-known flags create a brittle system that is deterministic and therefore easy to subvert.

The use of static lists of identities for security without randomization or comprehensive security tests requires both a flawless identity system and perfect knowledge of who will commit the next crime. Or, it creates a system with systematic flaws that are leveraged by criminals of all types, not just ideological criminal terrorists.

Consider the case of the no-fly list. If that were the sole protection, then by definition everyone who flies can be trusted. Of course, this is not the case. Every passenger is examined for metal and some for explosive residue. If the existence of an untrusted (and thus by default a more trusted) list decreases the overall scrutiny of each passenger or person not on the list, overall security is decreased. The least trusted person could obtain a false identifying information offering verification as the most trusted.

An identity-based security management system must be able to predict the source of the next attack. Otherwise, a person who has not yet implemented an attack but intends to do so can pass through the security system unchecked. A failure to predict the identity of the next attacker causes a failure in an identity-based system.

It is estimated that the Saudi terrorists spent millions of dollars and at least three years planning their attack on America 9/11. For $79.95, they could implement the same attack today:

A $79.95 Opportunity to Breeze Through Security

By JOE SHARKEY

NOT to put too fine a point on it, but I'd rather take a whack up the side of the head with a sack of cobblestones than wait in a long line to be treated badly when my turn comes.

This helps explain why I told Steve Brill last week to please take my $79.95 and sign me up. Mr. Brill, who founded Court TV and The American Lawyer magazine, is now the chief executive of a company called Verified Identity Pass. If Mr. Brill gets his way (and he usually does), his company's Clear Registered Traveler Program could soon have many members paying $79.95 each year to obtain an identity card that allows them to pass through airport checkpoints without being treated like a prisoner being hustled to the cellblock.

.....

Mr. Brill's program had about 7,000 enrolled members within a month after it started in mid-July, and he predicts it will have 10,000 "within a few weeks." Other pilot programs, which are administered by the Transportation Security Administration and don't charge a fee, are limited to 2,000 members at each participating airport.

What they all have in common is the means to let travelers identify themselves with a thin card encoded with their biometric data - iris and fingerprint scans - that the T.S.A. has checked against what Mr. Brill's company describes as "various terrorist-threat-related databases" and concluded that you have passed muster.

The reward for that is expedited passage through security in a designated lane, along with the assurance that you won't be randomly hauled aside for one of those secondary inspections and pat downs. Other future benefits, Mr. Brill said, might exempt travelers from much disliked rules like having to take off their shoes or remove laptops from their cases.

Identity is being used to confer trust. That sounds nice in an agrarian environment where identification implies knowledge. Yet in a networked environment where identity implies only authentication of a credential, trust based on identity makes no sense.

Could the Saudis, including a member of the large bin Ladin family, who were on the only non-military plane to take off September 12, be able to obtain an $80 card? If so, then the proposal increases rather than decreases risk by offering a security bypass to the most dangerous individuals.

Imagine that all Saudi's were denied this card. Than a tiny fraction of the millions of dollars could find someone who is highly trustworthy who never flies. That identity could then be used for travel, certain in the knowledge that the stolen identity purchases lower scrutiny. The criminal or attacker on the plane is the person who most values being trusted.

Consider the following examples of two parts of an institution protecting the same asset (people) against the same threat (car bombs).

The Kennedy School of Government occasionally host speakers from parts of the world characterized by protracted struggles with terrorists. The President of Turkey, the Prime Minister of the United Kingdom, and Benazir

Bhutto have each spoken there in the past few years. As such the Kennedy School is concerned with the threat of truck bombs.

One approach to this concern would be to check the identities of all drivers who approach the Kennedy School; another approach would refuse to allow any vehicle large enough to be a significant car bomb into the threat area. In fact, the Kennedy School of Government allows any vehicle to enter the parking area, but has installed large concrete "planters" that prevent any car from driving into the pedestrian or building areas.

Harvard University similarly considers itself a possible target for attack. Security at commencement was commensurate with this concern. Police officers were placed at every exit and entrance. During 2004 graduation cars were allowed into Harvard Yard lots based on the appearance of the driver. A female clad in rented academic robes was able to drive into parking areas in a Taurus wagon, with the back covered, with fully drivable access to the pavilion. The pavilion held the all the graduates of KSG and Harvard, with their respective esteemed families. The credentials confirmed were race of the driver, gender of the driver, and possession of academic robes.

The KSG approach is to protect against car bombs; the Harvard approach is to identify untrustworthy drivers. Thus under the Harvard College approach the driver must get past identity scrutiny only, and can do so cost the cost of a renting academic regalia.

KSG depends on specific *threat analysis* and *risk mitigation*. The Faculty of Arts and Science depends on *attribute authentication,* which imply some facts about identity.

The university example, CAPSS and CAPPS II illustrate the risks of using identity as a security management tool. The even more common use of trusting unauthenticated assertions of identity in risk management.

If only individuals who are known current or future threats are subject to scrutiny, then any unknown future criminal will escape security examination. This is a general observation, and applies to traffic stops as well as airline travel. One would expect that most criminals do not speed when there is a body in the trunk.

In the United States, there is currently no legislation or case law requiring identification to travel by air, because the courts are not hearing cases that assert the right to travel without identification. However, the Supreme Court has confirmed the right of a police officer to demand identification of any individual he or she approaches, *Hiibel v. Sixth Judicial Court of Nevada*. In this case the state claims that the ability to demand an unauthenticated claim of identity increases officer safety. This particular case is an excellent illustration of the misuse of identity in risk management.

For identification of a subject at the beginning of an interaction with police to be valuable requires three conditions. First, the identification must be accurate. Second, the identification must immediately correspond to useful attributes. Third, the identification and information must address an identified threat; thereby providing guidance for the officer that will immediately enhance his or her safety.

Without an authenticated identity leading to the corresponding appropriate response to the threat model, identification does not decrease risk. False identities, if believed, lull officers into believing that there is a low level of risk in a high-risk situation. If assertions of low risk identities cannot be believed, then the officer must always assume he or she is in a high-risk situation. The information cannot be trusted, and cannot be used in risk management. False identities used by dangerous suspects, and the resulting false sense of security by officers, may lead to an increase in risk. It is exactly the same as the airport searches; those who most need to be trusted (criminals) will invest more into trust-creating identities.

Without identity management as a risk tool, the implication is that every officer should treat every traffic stop and every encounter as potentially dangerous. Without identity management, every consumer should treat every web site as potentially dangerous and be careful about what information is being provided.

Demanding a claim of identity is demanding an identifier. "Are you a criminal?" offline. "Are you my bank?" online. "Are you my customer?" online.

The claim of identity is simply a claim of a label or credential. What is called identification is credential authentication. There is little or no direct way in which to confirm a simple claim of a name. In order to confirm the claim it will be necessary for the investigating officer to demand a list of associated claims that might authenticate the identity. For example, the officer would need to obtain date of birth and current address to confirm a claim of a name with driver's license records. In fact, the officer may need the drivers' license number itself depending upon the database access provided by the motor vehicle provider to confirm the claim. The criminal who is emptying a bank account will have the victim's Social Security Number and the victim's mother's birthday handy. The criminal will never forget your mother's birthday on the phone with customer service. However, you might.

Asking for a name is either asking for a completely unverified and therefore useless label from a potentially hostile party, or asking for a data set that verifies any claim of identity. A completely unverified claim of identity is of no use in a criminal situation. Increasingly, the unverified claims of identity using public information online are useless. An innocent party will provide correct information while any suspicious party would mis-identify.

Criminal aliases were used before identity management systems in law enforcement, and their value to criminals in fraud and detection is well documented.

Imagine that an unchangeable biometric, such as fingerprints, is embedded on the diver's license or used at a remote site for online access. Once fingerprints are available in a driver license database, those data are then available for theft and misuse. If the stolen information is from a person with no previous criminal record then any possible record could be added – there will be no extant data and the goal of the criminal will simply be to have a match. Utilizing real time biometrics requires highly available networked technology. The evaluator would have to be able to observe the collection of the fingerprint. Then a database search would reveal identity if there was a match. With current field technology, innocent individuals will be denied access, and criminals will escape, as data capture technologies have not evolved to the point where those who are not technologists will have reliable, consistent reads. If the technology were to ever be so mature, then there would be a possible trade of privacy for security. Under current social, organizational and technical conditions, privacy is lost and security is decreased.

Even given the ideal technologies, the treatment of all interactions as potentially dangerous is the best possible practice for the police officer as well as the consumer, for the same reason that the treatment of all patients as bearing infectious disease is the best possible medical practice. In both cases, those identified as previously benign may suddenly change to hazardous. In both cases, professional practice of self-protection and wariness is the best defense for the professional on the front lines.

Identity systems that function best are those that identify an individual through an un-forgeable biometric (the capture of which is observed by law enforcement and processed appropriately) that is linked to a specific attribute. The use of other identity management tools has abetted criminals in committing fraud, escaping justice, and evading surveillance. Identity systems are best used only when the threat is one of misidentification, rather than for attribute forgery.

4. Who Owns You?

Identity is not about who you are. Identity management does not determine if you are a good person, or bad. It is rather the processes that allow actions and decisions, and determine the set of opportunities that people have given how identity is constructed. "Identity management" is actually a set of products to address a set of problems.

Identity in the digital realm is far less about who you are and more about what will be offered or done to you. Identity is not about you as subject, but you as object: to whom, from whom, by whom and for whom. Understanding your role as idealized by the construction of the identity means being able to navigate the various identity constructions.

Identity in the digital realm determines essential choices, even more freedoms. Identity among individuals is personal, with identity depending on the relationship with the individual: professional, paternal, casual, hostile and every combination of these that exists. If you have more resources and are more able pay then you will be charged more. Identity construction in a digital age is not relationship or personalization, it is pricing and determination of options.

Identity management is focused on fraud prevention and detection, in the sense of "identity theft". Identity theft is also an issue of payment, determining is a payment is valid. These are what individuals think of when it comes to identity threat.

Identity management is much more than that for vendors. Digital rights management is about control of users, more than payment. Vendors want not only payment for use; vendors also want to sell specific business plans. Certainly music providers can make money with paid music downloads. Yet there is much music that simply cannot be purchased. There are historical movies that cannot be rented, but must be obtained in a traditional (unusable) format because the copyright owner is not known. There are copyright owners who have an antipathy towards the Internet and thus never want the material on the net. So this is not simply an issue of payment, but of access. The argument over DRM is an argument over ownership, access, and creativity of culture.

Identity management is an issue of resource allocation. What privileges do you have? Do you have the deluxe cable configuration?

Identity management enables personalization and price discrimination.

Finally identity management is about filtering. Did Hillary Clinton shoot Vince Foster and drag his body to the park? Obviously not. Were there weapons of mass destruction in Iraq? The answer is a documented negative. However, there are people who believe this. There is a strong market in providing them with only the news with which they will agree. In order to provide information services, including news, as consumer-defined rather than fact-based requires knowing a tremendous amount about the consumer. But even in this case you need not know "who" the user is. What you need to know is a credential that indicates a particular life view.

There are two basic identifiers: the set of public information including name and date of birth, and the ability to respond to an email.

Me@WhereIAm

Email is the network identifier, the new "family name". Last names on the net are domain names. A person is not longer a member of a good family, but an AOL working stiff or a Gmail high school student.

There are authenticated emails, such as my own jean_camp@harvard.edu. That email provides a name, and attaches the name to an institution that has a well-known name and a reputation to protect. Hopefully, the organization does not give out emails at random but only grants emails to people somehow affiliated with the organization. In this context, affiliated means being paid by, giving money to, graduating from, or providing services to Harvard University. However, anecdotal evidence indicates that this authentication is limited as one project director allegedly managed to keep an email address for four years after being fired from the University. My email address is still valid, in my third year at Indiana University because I am officially on leave. In fact, I am simply affiliated as a courtesy until my doctoral students graduate. If you went to Harvard for enforcement against an action taken by me, there would be little response. (Of course the institution could cancel the email address.)

There then are weakly authenticated emails. I have one of these as well, me@ljean.org. This domain is authenticated based on the information provided in the database of information of those who own domain names.

The degree to which domain names are linked to identity has been a subject of passionate debate for several years. The body developed to be a technically coordinating committee for domain names has been deeply immersed in this very political issue. The Internet Corporation for the Assignment of Names and Numbers (ICANN) is a self-selected group of the technical elite that is optimal for a technical standards-setting body but quite ill-suited to discuss issues of identity, anonymity, and privacy. Therefore there is no way to predict the final association of domain names and identity. Some advocate passionately for the right to speak anonymously on the Internet. Others, so alarmed by the explosion of spam and the widespread illegal sharing of information subject to copyright, passionately oppose anonymity. Those in the first group want to be certain that individuals can broadcast information without threat from oppressive governments, violent extremists, and organized crime. Those in the second category want to make certain that law enforcement can identify and punish those who commit illegal acts on the Internet. Unfortunately, there is quite a bit of overlap between a repressive government and its police forces, and law enforcement is not immune to the charms of illegal profit or even the siren songs of extreme rhetoric.

Domain names offer some opportunity to keep our roles distinct. Our choices in identity depend on the people who own valuable mass produced content. This intellectual property lobby wants to make more money by giving people less – fewer ways to play and use what is bought, and no right to use names that the product designers have declared property. The likely result of their efforts is mandatory email portability, rather than eternal customer lock-in. Yet the delay between the costs of implementing email portability and the profits to be made with lock-in ensures the continued closure of the domain name market.

Email Trust-Based Viruses

"I love you," said the heading of the email. How could you not answer that? If the person emailing were your boss, it would be frightening, intriguing or simply disgusting. Perhaps that particularly proper executive or colleague with whom you have had an arms-length relationship underlined with the secret longing that has given so much to novels these many centuries.

The "love bug" was the first virus to take explicit advantage of what was only implied with all the previous attacks that used only the victim's address books – computer viruses are social things. They thrive on our connections to each other. Like a physical virus they spread from contact. Here we will describe how an email virus like and unlike a physical virus.

Email viruses can be thought of in many different ways, each way implies a different response both from society as a whole and from the end user. These mental models of email viruses may be useful in understanding risks in computer systems.

There are four popular ways to think about viruses: as an infection of the system, as a crime, as an economic outcome to optimal investment, and as war. Each model has different behavioral implication. Embracing whatever model is appropriate can help you develop your own effective behaviors and heuristics without requiring risk calculus for each interaction. These models can be used, as a whole, to effectively understand the mental models of computer scientists. With an organization, these models can guide security policy, and be used to provide a checklist for computer security for managers who need not know the technical details.

Mental models may be useful in communicating risk within the security communities, but they can communicate perverse as well as effective incentives. Thus both possible types of messages are described here. When experts use models and metaphors in their own explanations and understanding of systems, the metaphors are used to explain a particular element of a system based on a common understanding. When experts communicate to non-experts then those who are not expert then those end users take more than is intended by the expert. Therefore the use of these models in organizational educational programs must be considered carefully.

Many of the practices abandoned by environmental scientists continue to be used in attempt to communicate risk to computer users. These include enumerating all possible risks, attempting to make all those exposed to risk experts in the subject manner, and the use of confusing metaphors with potentially perverse implications.

Possible Solutions

The human element is the core of confidence scams, so any solution to the proliferation of must have this element at its core. The range of extant security technologies can solve the problems of impersonation in a technical sense; however these have failed in the larger commercial and social context. Computers excel at communication of data; calculation of complex reputations; and offer consistent interfaces. Computers cannot judge context. People can make subtle distinctions based on context: to calculate, differentiate and evaluate specific unique computers. In contrast, humans make decisions by lumping, simplification, and evaluation of context. People are asked to function as if they were computers in the design of many security systems.

Internet commerce is embedded in daily life. According to a study conducted by Pew Internet & American Life Project (PEW), online banking increased 127%, online auction participation has doubled, and e-purchasing expanded by 63% from 2000 to 2002, respectively (PEW, 2002a). As the popularity and prevalence of e-commerce transactions has increased so have malicious and fraudulent activities. As the criminal use of technologies has become more sophisticated, it has become substantially more difficult to evaluate web merchants.

Attacks are increasing social as well as physical. For example, common fraudulent activities come in the form of unscrupulous merchants and "phishing" sites. In the digital age, new types of fraudulent activities have emerged, such as "phishing" scams. A phishing site impersonates a trusted entity, for example a consumer's bank, in order to attain personally identifiable information. Such information includes passwords and account numbers, credit card numbers, and social security numbers.

Well before the instantiation of e-commerce, merchant fraud was a popular and profitable endeavor (e.g., PEW 2002b). Unscrupulous merchant practices include everything from the ill-mannered (misleading the consumer about the product quality), to the irresponsible (collecting and selling personally identifiable information) to the illegal (charging the consumer twice). Merchant misinformation is not unique to the Internet. However, the ease of masquerading attacks and ability to construct false business facades are so different in quantitative terms that there is also arguably a qualitative change. While there exists a range of security protocols that are a testament to the brilliance of their creators, Internet-based confidence scams are in fact increasing in popularity and sophistication as organized crime has become involved.

The Federal Trade Commission has reported that in 2004, 53% of all fraud complaints were Internet-related with identity theft at the top of the complaint list with 246,570 complaints, up 15 percent from last year. (FTC, 2004) PEW has noted that 68% of Internet users surveyed were concerned about criminals obtaining their credit card information, while 84% were worried that their personal information would be compromised. (PEW, 2002b)

Banking institutions, Federal law, and criminal courts distinguish between these various sources and types of fraud. There are significant legal distinctions between instantiations of unauthorized use of authenticating information to assert identity in the financial namespace. Yet the risk for the subject of information is the same regardless of the mechanisms of disclosure. For example, when Choicepoint exposed 145,000 California users to an identity thief, it was because one criminal created 43 authorized accounts. Choicepoint created no legal violation, as a data brokers have no privacy constraints. The business model, not the security protocols, of Choicepoint is itself the threat to American consumers. When Bank of America lost unencrypted back-up tapes of personal account information that included 1.2M records this was a security failure based on a flawed policy. When personnel information was stolen from a laptop at the University of California at Berkeley, it was theft of property and the existence of personal information on the laptop was a violation of university security policy. While policymakers should make these distinctions, there is no reason for any victim of theft from these incidents to make this distinction. The end result was the same. Similarly end users have been given a proliferation of tools that distinguish between privacy policies (Privacy Bird), key hierarchies (PKI), and some of which identify malicious sites of a certain category (e.g., PhishGuard). But there has not been a unified system that leverages peer production of consumer knowledge to evaluate risks in all its forms – legal and otherwise. The proposed system integrates privacy threats, security threats, masquerading attacks, and threats such as alignment of business model against the customers' interests. Individuals need not make these specific decisions and evaluate individual's computers but rather to obtain integrated and aggregated risk information and thus make informed decisions.

Federated Identity

In the early days of telephony one important social question was how to greet the individual on the other end of the line. Some social creativity was necessary because with the telephone people had not been introduced. Without being introduced; how could one know how to greet another? The standard greetings, sire, sir, madam or miss, could become sources of embarrassment.

There were two proposals, one from sailing traditions, "ahoy". The other was, "hallo", a term used originally to mean, "Halt!" or "Cease". By the time of its introduction to telephony, it had become a generic cry to obtain general attention.

As "hello" became the universal introduction, so Liberty Alliance seeks to become the universal introducer. Yet "hello" is fundamentally a personal greeting Liberty Alliance is constructed to allow corporations to pass bits of authentication around about individuals. Standards function at different levels of complexity, with "hello" above being an example of the most simple. The Liberty Alliance conceptualizes itself as an introduction service; yet because of the amount of data that can be transferred it would better be compared with the traditional informal gossip network than the introduction service.

The Liberty Alliance is a set of standards and definitions, and more importantly assumptions about types of interactions. The fundamental assumption in the Liberty Alliance standard is that are sets of groups that define certain credentials (e.g., over 18, a student, a member of a professional association). There is another, sometimes overlapping set of groups that depend on those credentials (e.g., wine merchants, publishers). Finally there are individuals who interact with both groups.

The core fundamental goal of the Liberty Alliance is to allow business to affiliate their employees with internal roles; and then share the information about the employee's role to other corporate affiliates. The ability to share customer data is valuable; yet the core construction of Liberty Alliance is to provide cross-enterprise communication about employees.

Just as people use greetings today without considering the history, people will be using Liberty Alliance without being aware of the interaction. Liberty Alliance is expected to have one billion devices and accounts in 2006.

The Liberty Alliance is built on the concept of a *circle of trust*. The circle of trust is in fact a network of data-sharing hierarchies. Each hierarchy has a core authenticating entity. That authenticator (or *identity provider* in the parlance of Liberty Alliance) verifies the credentials of an individual. Then, with those credentials, the individual can make assertions about his or her rights or account status to any entity in the circle of trust. Each circle of trust accepts a set of credentials. The ability of the individual to prevent leakage between circles is based on limitations of data sharing (which are contractual) and credential queries.

Liberty, as a standard, cannot constrain the storage, compilation or use of data once the data are shared. The criticism of the Liberty Alliance standard is that it vastly simplifies data sharing across discrete enterprises at a per-transaction level. By signing on with a single identity provider a person commits to trust a large number of entities. By linking accounts as disparate sites, the person is deciding to inform all the sites of her activities as she crosses multiple locations. Of course, web bugs and cookies do such tracking today. In contrast with the current tracking of companies such as DoubleClick, the Liberty Alliance does provide values to the person being tracked.

The Liberty Alliance is, as it has been widely adopted, a technology to tie together discrete PKI instantiations in a manner that is meaningful for the members of the discrete organizations. The Liberty Alliance can allow a company to identify employees of its suppliers, it subsidiaries, and employees of business partners.

Liberty Alliance definitions vary from those commonly used, with *traits* being the equivalent of *attributes*. Liberty Alliance considers an identity as that that which distinguishes the user. This definition makes identification and authentication equivalent.

Liberty Alliance the standard has been the basis for a family of products built to comply with those open standards. Liberty Alliance has as its basis a set of authentication and identification mechanisms that need to interact. The interaction of these hierarchies creates a network of hierarchies.

Liberty Alliance also offers businesses that are in a circle of trust the opportunity for non-authenticated anonymous data requests. For example, a weather service may want to check for zip code, and set that as the user's base zip code. However, there is no reason to further authenticate any requests for information about weather by constraining the zip code. There is no threat model of zip code misrepresentation at weather sites. There is a need to check alternative zip codes (obviously for travel).

When an individual who is part of the Liberty Alliance begins a session that individual signs into a particular sphere defined by a shared identity space. A single sign-on to the web services framework initiates a Liberty Identity session. That session is authenticated with a party that will verify claims about an individual's identity and attributes. In the circle of trust model of Liberty Alliance, this entity is called an "identity provider". What is provided is not, of course, an identity by rather authentication of a set of claimed attributes. The individual begins interacting with the services referencing the identity provider who authenticates attributes, so the now-authenticated individual can access a set of services. The ability of different entities to authenticate various attributes is what enables the individual's experience of single sign-on, and more importantly, single sign-off. One individual can exist in multiple domains, with the trust domain defined by the identity provider.

A potential issue with the Liberty Alliance is that it is not the choice of the identified person what data are shared. In theory the individual would have distinct identities in each circle of trust. To the extent that there is overlap the single identity of an employee, a political volunteer, a family member, and a gamer becomes one person with little privacy or control over personal data. Liberty Alliance both offers single sign-on, and threatens to remove the ability to segregate our identities. For example, one person with an employee identifier in the Hilton may add associations via the Hilton. Association information available from the Hilton may include a political gathering (e.g., YearlyKos, Focus on the Family), an employment fair, a family vacation, or a gamer conference. All of these identities and details may be available to members of the Hilton circle of trust, depending upon the policies of the corporate partners.

John Deere provides a model use of Liberty Alliance. John Deere owns it manufacturing facilities, has a network of suppliers, a corporate sales force, and a network of individual retail dealers. With Liberty Alliance, John Deere can allow individual retailers to set the rights of individuals to make purchases or enter records while still identifying each person uniquely during that interaction. John Deere does not have to make any changes at the corporate IT system as the dealers and suppliers experience employee turnover. Because John Deere is but one "identity provider" it addressed enrollment of partners, who then enroll and authenticate their own employees. Enrollment is distributed to the corporation or its partners. Each business entity is responsible for the actions of those it has enrolled. Verification is handled by the business or business unity. Recovery is similarly distributed.

The Liberty Alliance is built to implement data protection policies, as the standards includes mechanisms for user approval of data sharing and, in some cases, auditing of data use. Liberty Alliance documentation illustrates examples of systems that enable pseudonyms, as well as illustrating client interactions to empower individuals over data sharing. However, at its core, Liberty Alliance is a business-centric mechanism built to simplify corporate cooperation and data sharing. To the extent that privacy is the opposite of price discrimination, the promise of the standard is unlikely to be implemented in practice.

Single sign-up is enabled within a circle of trust and across circles of trust. Yet the highest level of the hierarchy defines the circle of trust. This is not a circle where we all fall back into each other's hands. This is a circle that risks allowing many hands to easily reach in and pull out our wallets, examining our photos of our children along with our employer ID.

Liberty Alliance authentication can be strong or weak; however, federation inevitably has some element of centralization and is built to be eventually ubiquitous. To the extent that the circles of trust do not overlap, Liberty Alliance offers a strong, decentralized but interoperable mechanism for sharing credentials and identifiers. Like CardSpace, Liberty Alliance is a privacy-neutral or privacy-enabling technology being constructed in an economic environment that is hostile to privacy.

CardSpace

CardSpace, the identity management platform integrated into Microsoft Vista, is compatible with the Liberty Alliance. CardSpace is the mechanism for the consumer to interact with the range of Federated Identities in various spheres of trust that are predicted to arise.

CardSpace, formally known as InfoCard, is a neutral technology to allow storage of a set of credentials in each individual's machine under their own username. Because of the technical control over the credentials by the user, CardSpace is neutral in the types of technology that is allowed. CardSpace can support anonymous credentials as well as known credentials. Similarly, CardSpace can support demands from sites that you provide all credentials.

CardSpace is not instantiated with credentials from Microsoft. CardSpace may be moved to embed credentials from Microsoft, for example for the purpose of limiting services to those using Microsoft products without a current license. CardSpace can store credentials provided by any entity that follows the standard.

CardSpace also enables individuals to create their own credentials, presumably out of information such a shipping address and contact information. If you provide a retailer with an incorrect shipping address, then you are the one who does not receive your package.

Card Space follows the laws of identity. Recall the laws are:

Human integration simply means that the interaction is usable. Clicking on one icon means the same as clicking on another icon in the same window.

CardSpace follows these laws. The data subject as controller of the mouse is not adequate for privacy. CardSpace does reduce reliance on password

CardSpace allows what it calls self-asserted identities. Self-asserted attributes can include identifying information or simply be anonymous credentials. The credentials are stored locally. These credentials are not corroborated, and usually mean "I am the same person who came to this web site last week." These are often used for preferences, blogs, free email accounts portals and other unauthenticated interactions.

One goal of CardSpace is to "improve the accuracy of data". To the extent that the only option individuals often have when facing a request for information is to provide incorrect information, CardSpace limits individual autonomy. Anyone who has ever lied to share a credential at the New York

Times or deny information to a demanding web merchant will be unable to use this strategy in the future.

CardSpace runs on the trusted computing base. This means it is more secure than other processes, like Word or Safari. It is isolated from Windows desktop.   It uses self-assigned graphical passwords, so a person can personalizes a card with their own individual icon.

CardSpace will allow fast checkout. So instead of filling out every form, there is an automated mechanism for filling out forms. This does mean if you want to create different identities with self-asserted credentials ("consultant", "girl scout leader"). However, if you want to send random misinformation (for example, companies that require your employment information) this is made more difficult.

CardSpace permits the use of one-time passwords and thus has the potential to limit identity theft. CardSpace is most certainly not a privacy-enhancing product. It is at best a privacy-neutral product. When it is placed in the marketplace there is no incentive for any party to minimize information collection.

In terms of incentives, there is no reason for every merchant not to ask for the most possible information. Every merchant can obtain your self-signed credentials by asking the user, or simply requiring the largest scope of information.   Today, you would not be able to send the credentials from Amazon to Barnes and Noble to the extent that they are embedded in cookies. Amazon could easily ask for blog credentials, in order to improve their marketing and know where to advertise.

The information of these cards must be pulled out from an identity provider. In practice there are four or five identity providers if this catches on. So a user is always connected to the identity provider when they transact. There is, for most authentication actions in CardSpace, there is a third party watching you actions. Now, instead of Amazon and you knowing that you connect to Amazon there will be an oracle that knows whenever you authenticate to any site.

CardSpace will include governmental information to the extent that the individual interacts with the government. Do you have a credential from the parole board? Do you have taxpayer credential or a credential that allows you to pay your property tax? If the average person is offered a few cents off for sharing credentials, most will do it.

Certainly it is unlikely that anyone would know his or her many-digit Amazon user unique identification number. CardSpace is built so that privacy enhancing technologies can be added. Yet what is already built in is the sharing of information, not the protection of privacy. Yet the incentives in the market, the lack of legal protection, and the default settings make CardSpace could be a user-centric privacy disaster, or the perfect privacy platform. The technology is arguably neutral. The economic incentives are not. Yet CardSpace will increase the ease of information sharing and the velocity of information without privacy defaults. The combination of increased speed of information sharing, strong economic incentives against privacy, and no default high-privacy settings makes CardSpace a reason for concern.

CardSpace is built to simplify the sharing of identity information and credentials. To share your name and address, you need to provide the information being shared. You may have to fill out a form, if the browser does not recognize the site. With CardSpace, you can share all your affiliations and identity information with the click of a button.

I could generate "Jean" credentials for CardSpace that indicate if you have previously been to ljean.com. I could do the same, more easily with cookies. However, with CardSpace other sites could then easily access that credential. I could also ask, without generating credentials, for you to check a "yes" box so that I could read every credential in CardSpace. Just by visiting the page and swatting a dialogue box, a site that once passively obtained network address information can now may be able to read credentials and attributes. In the worst case, merchants can check affiliations, zip code (a rich source of statistical data), and the implicit information embedded in our names.

By increasing the ease of sharing, the ease of compilation, and the velocity of information sharing CardSpace is not privacy neutral. CardSpace is neutral on privacy in the way that an egg on the edge of a counter is neutral on cleanliness. The very nature of the technology, combined with the motivations of the merchants and the policy vacuum, mean that CardSpace risks exacerbate privacy violations and identity theft.

Microsoft ID Card

Now we move from the realm of current products and Vista press releases into the domain of grand plans as described by white papers in the Microsoft research domain. Vista is a product, designed to market and thus marketable by design. As universal identifiers become acceptable under the RealID implementation, Microsoft will be ready. Microsoft research proposes a Tamper-Resistant Biometric ID Card that reads into a Microsoft Tamper-Resistant Biometric ID Card Reader and then is evaluated with the Tamper-Resistant Biometric ID Card verification software. Microsoft is seeking to market this as a national ID card; and in particular has presented strong opposition to the current designs of the UK National Identity card. (See (Microsoft Research 2006a; Microsoft research 2006b) for more details.)

With the Microsoft Biometric ID Card there is an initial imprimatur of a fingerprint onto a smart card. (The choice of fingerprints limits the population for which the card is effective.) Then to complete enrollment, data are associated with the smart card in the complementary centralized component. The card holds asymmetric cryptographic protocols that are then used for authentication for the enrolled identity.

The documentation on the Microsoft ID card indicates that the card is a neutral component of a larger identity system. Indeed there is not reason not to use the Microsoft ID card for unique personal identification to a Liberty Alliance Identity Provider.

The documentation states that all information is held on the card, and all information can be recovered if the card is lost. This indicates that the data must be backed up using some either standard database or a secure cryptographic mechanism. Either is possible but not inherent to the Card or its infrastructure.

It is reasonable to assume that the strategic goal of the Microsoft ID card is to create a secure connection between the customer and the company that will mitigate the inherent advantage of any other party in identity management. Failing to publish critical interface information has been used by Microsoft (for example, early on in its terminate and stay resident TSR) to leverage its operating system monopoly. More recently, Microsoft attempted to implement a version of Kerberos that is incompatible with Apache. No such activities have been reported with respect to the MS ID Card.

It is the fiscal responsibility of any company to leverage its assets. Microsoft's greatest asset is its ownership of the desktop. Future integration would risk privileging Microsoft appliances. The card-based secure hardware push maybe targeted at the proliferation of Linux, LAMP and Mozilla (particularly in the server market).

The success of this potentially strong and decentralized ID system depends on effective enrollment and organization. Recall that in biometric terms enrollment is the ability to connect the biometric being used for identification and the party identified. (Biomterics are described in more detail in Chapter 12.) Once biometric data are on the network they are simply data and can be captured like any other data.

The MS ID Card removes the biometric data from the network, and has the card itself authenticate the associated biometric.

Microsoft leaves issues of conflicts, failures to enroll, and claims to multiple identities by one biometric, and enrollment to other partners. In this way the MS ID Card is a platform for any party to adopt and use. This also enables different organizations to have different practices in terms of security, based on the particular organization's risk profile. Because the biometric is one the card, failure in one organization may not easily cascade to other domains.

The Microsoft InfoCard is a system that does not include biometrics on the hardware but is a similar platform to the Biometric ID card in strategic terms. Again the enrollment is a function of a third party, as are protection, verification, and recovery.

Microsoft's ID Card and InfoCard are bound with other elements of the long-delayed Longhorn/Vista platform, e.g., Indigo the Longhorn messaging system and the Avalon presentation system. Integration with

Avalon provides an opportunity for future DRM opportunities, with guarantees on the Microsoft client/server structure.

By entering attributes into the card, Microsoft would then have the capacity to be a secure attribute broker between any entities that utilize the card. Smart cards which require individual authentication enable a dedicated, strong, and decentralized system. Smart cards with centralized and vulnerable centralized data storage can also enable a ubiquitous, centralized and thus vulnerable system.

Real ID

The Real ID system was approved in 2005 as a rider to a bill after having been defeated as a stand-alone bill for many years. RealID requires that every state create a database interoperable with every other state's database. RealID requires that every state issue driver's licenses that have a format that is readable by a standard reader.

There are two core organizational problems with the RealID Act: initiation and recovery.

Initiation is enrollment in the RealID scheme. RealID requires more than a driver license to renew a driver's license. For example, RealID requires a passport or a birth certificate. Birth certificates can be problematic, particularly for the elderly. The elderly have greater difficulty obtaining birth certificates first because of the simple passage of time. Those born long ago are more likely to be born at hospitals that may have closed than those born recently. Secondly, the centralization of medical care and state record keeping that has occurred during the twentieth century may have missed small, community hospitals. Finally, the elderly will not have living parents who may have maintained that documentation. Also, not everyone born in the past 75 years had been issued a birth certificate. Some states (e.g., Missouri) allows one to certify birth by having two RealID-bearing individuals come to swear that you were born to them. While this can address recent home births, the elderly are unlikely to have this option.

Secondly, RealID is flawed because of recovery issues. If an identity thief obtains a RealID before the victim does, then the ID theft victim will have great difficulty asserting her valid identity. Should a criminal choose to use another's identity as an alias, then that criminal will know that obtaining a RealID in some state is time critical. The victim, who may be living in another state, will be oblivious to the need to race to get a verified identified.

RealID has design problems. RealID is not secure for a digital environment, e.g., not cryptographically secure. This means that anyone who has all your RealID data can construct a convincing fraudulent RealID. To the extent that this false RealID is trusted the RealID will enable identity theft, and criminal use of trusted identities as aliases.

Secretary Chernoff has announced that RealID compliance is to be out-sourced to data aggregators. Thus, individuals are at risk for having their verified identities questioned based on a refusal to accurately fill out web forms. Sen. Lieberman (CFL-CN) notes that RealID will not enhance security, "because it is overly burdensome, possibly unworkable, and may actually increase a terrorist's ability to commit identity theft." (Hsu and Fears, 2007).

RealID is effectively a national identity card requirement, with the cost of the card moved to the states. The states, as well as civil liberty organizations, oppose the plan. Libertarians oppose the plan because of the information embedded in card. Conservatives oppose the plan because the amount of information on the card. For example, should the card contain all state data then a driver with a gun permit in Maine may face increased scrutiny when his RealID is read in Boston.

In January 2006, both Houses of the State Legislature of Maine passed a joint resolution to prohibiting the state from participating in RealID. Part of the reason for this resistance is the discovery of the cost, which has estimates running from tens to hundreds of millions. Other states in which such resolutions are pending include Georgia, New Hampshire, Washington, New Mexico, and Hawaii. The combination of states indicates that the combination of unfunded mandate and civil liberty violation has opponents across the political spectrum. There are 21 states[5] that have adopted or are debating the rejection of the RealID. The National Governors Association objects to Real ID as an "$11 billion unfunded mandate". (Hsu and Fears, 2007)

Ironically, New Jersey appears to support RealID despite the increased value and risk of false licenses. New Jersey has a particularly colorful history of false identifications; with the purchase and creation of state documents appearing to be something of a local industry. For example, the entire staff of the Newark office was fired in 2003; as an investigation found that corruption was rampant at all levels of the office. (CDT, 2003) RealID critically depends upon honesty and integrity at the issuing agency. Thus it is particularly problematic that there exists regular detection of corruption as documented at http://www.cdt.org/privacy/030131motorvehicle.shtml

At the Federal level the instantiation of standards enables the adoption of new and improved identity mechanisms, mechanisms that can work online as well as off. The technologies described in the following chapters (identity-based cryptography, secure hardware, anonymous credentials) can enable secure authentication suitable for the digital age, impossible to forge, and privacy-enhancing. This would be more expensive

---

[5] This is as of January 2007.

both at the Federal and individual lever, as privacy-sensitive individuals would need to purchase the appropriate readers for their computers.

Senators Sununu (R-NH) and Akaka (D-HI) have introduced a bi-partisan bill for the 2005 session to replace the RealID set of requirements with a process of developing optimal technical standards.

Implications of Different Identity Management Systems

The same core problems apply to all identity management systems: enrollment, protection, verification, and recovery. These are different by degrees in the different systems.

Enrollment is the process of associating a particular identification or authentication mechanism with a particular social identity or attribute. My fingerprint needs to be entered into a database as being associated with me or it is, in the larger context, meaningless. The Vehicle ID number on my car must be entered into a database that corresponds to ownership data, location of registration, and insurance history. Identifiers are only as useful, ever, as enrollment is effective.

Verification is the true strength of most identity systems. If enrollment were successful, there has been no change of status, and no failures; identity management systems are highly successful at verification of claims of attributes or identities.

Recovery is also essential. Data concentration in identity systems creates the opportunity for catastrophic system failure. An excellent example is the loss of Bank of America backup data, which contained the account and authenticating information for every retail customer.

Data distribution using phones or cards itself is less risky than concentration in a centralized database in terms of system-wide recovery. Of course, for decentralized back-up with no real-time access, data can be easily stored in a manner such that the failure of any one database, either in terms of loss of integrity or confidentiality, that no data are lost. In this case, recovery may necessarily be linked to enrollment, as recovery becomes secondary enrollment.

Every identity system, in fact every security system, is a denial of service mechanism waiting to happen[6]. Identity theft, where the victim cannot travel or obtain credit, can be seen as a highly personalized form of denial of service. Defense from denial of service attacks is a critical dimension of recovery.

---

[6] A denial of service attack is one where rather than hijacking or subverting resources; attackers implement an attack that has as a goal and strategy of exhausting the resources of the victim (e.g., filling up the bandwidth) so the victim is unable to function.

Protection is the degree to which an identifier requires protection, and the particular threats of an information system. Protection includes protection from threats to availability, data integrity and confidentiality.

When there is a loss of confidentiality in identity information, the result is a breach of privacy. In some cases, there is a corresponding breach of security.

Strangely, most authenticating information is, in fact, a matter of public record. Marriage and birth records are public records. A birth record can be traced to a marriage record, thus the attribute mother's maiden name can be determined from public records. For identity systems to be secure, the identifying information must be confidential and private.

Verification is the confirmation of a claim of identity. Identity theft is based on a failure of verification. The correct person initially enrolls, yet another person is able to verify the (false) identity. For example, in the United States data brokers provide much of the information that is used by individuals for verification.

A loss in integrity in information can be more challenging than a loss of confidentiality. In the loss of integrity case, the data are no longer reliable. When data are no longer available, then there is no basis for authentication of claimed identities. When data lose integrity, then the basis for authentication is itself incorrect.

Centralized and distributed systems have very distinct failure modes. Centralized systems are more likely to suffer catastrophic failure, while distributed systems failures must cascade to create significant difficulties. Keeping data consistent is more difficult in a distributed system; yet data loss can be more problematic in a centralized system. Because of the difference in threats, there are corresponding differences in recovery.

Centralized systems also have a significant failure mode: criminals masquerade as the authorized party. Different mechanisms fall under the names phishing, pharming, advance fee fraud, and 419 frauds. All are cases of masquerade attacks, where a criminal entity presents themselves as trustworthy using a combination of human tendencies to trust, and the systematic technical and organizational failures that plague our ill-considered identity infrastructure.

5.   Defeating the Greatest Masquerade

Identity theft, phishing, identity fraud, criminal identity theft and payment instrument frauds are all examples of malicious activity that requires a successful masquerade. Even confidence fraud is a masquerade, of a criminal who claims to be an honest person in a particularly difficult or powerful situation. Why networks and databases have made it more difficult to maintain privacy, these technologies have also conversely made masquerade attacks easier. An examination of masquerade attacks can illuminate the importance of credentials, the threats that together create identity theft, and the relationship between privacy and security.

In the real-world context, an individual evaluates the amount of perceived risk in a specific context through familiarity of social and physical context. People infer knowledge about someone's "values and moral commitments on the basis of their clothing, behavior, general demeanor … or a common background". (Kim & Prabhakar 2002) An individual will trust another individual or a merchant if the other person is significantly similar to them; the similarity and hence perceived familiarity "triggers trusting attitudes". (Kim & Prabhakar 2002; Kalakota et. al., 1997) Online, those social cues are absent.

Web Spoofing and Scams

Following is a false PayPal Web page. This type of masquerade attack is called phishing. Phishing is possible because, despite the efforts in identifying consumers to merchants, there is less information for consumers to identify the merchants in return.

The lack of a proper Internet address may identify this as a scam, yet in the email the link to the address will say http://www.paypal.com. And of course a higher quality fraud would add the image of the lock and the image of the correct URL.

Note that a core part of the business plan of PayPal is to avoid the cost of fraud implemented over its payment system. For example, by using bank accounts rather than credit cards, PayPal makes disputing fraud more difficult and pays less overhead for fraud management. Thus risk is shifted to the consumer.

Unlike PayPal, this website requests a Social Security Number. Of course, one should never ever provide a Social Security Number over email or web pages. This masquerade attack is taking advantage of the fact that PayPal has convinced its customers to enter their banking information. By obtaining access to a bank account through the PayPal password, the attacker can transfer funds to his or her own account. Unlike with credit card theft, the victim loses those funds forever. By obtaining a SSN, the attacker can implement another set of masquerade attacks.

First the attacker masquerades as PayPal to the customers of PayPal. Second, the attackers use the information from the phishing attack to obtain new accounts in false names. The individuals who fall for this attack are victimized at least twice. First the victims lose access to established accounts. Second, the victims may be held responsible for accounts opened in their names by the attackers.

The ability to misuse individual information and the importance of never sharing a SSN underscore that fact that privacy is security.

Figure 1: An Attack on PayPal Customers Using Identity Confusion

The belief that lack of privacy will make us more secure is the underlying mechanism that allows these frauds to succeed.

Notice that there is no browser lock, indicating that SSL is not in use. Therefore, in addition to the criminals implementing the masquerade attacks, all information entered on this web page is transmitted unprotected. Therefore any group of criminals (they need not be affiliated with the phishing attack) could read the information from the Web form as it crosses the network.

In fact the Security Sockets Layer[7] (SSL) security system can be undermined. Criminals can obtain legitimate certificates. If the criminal is willing to pay for the certificate, the criminal can obtain one. Certainly these criminals are masters of identity theft, so they will have the information of a trustworthy person. They can use this to purchase a certificate with a domain that appears trustworthy. For example, an organization calling itself paypal.unfraud.com obtained thousands of valid credit cards through its trustworthy name and fine interface. Another way to obtain a certificate is to have a boring domain name, such as "cgi.com". The domain name will be sent to the victim as http://www.paypal.com.login.usr.bin.cgi.com/

One recent variation of phishing spam targets people by sending mail as if "from" the victim to bogus accounts. So the user opens his mailbox and finds a list of replies from email he hasn't sent. Emails like this:

To :unlucky@isp.net

Subject : Undelivered Mail Returned to Sender

From :MAILER-DAEMON@cs.uni-potsdam.de (Mail Delivery System)

I'm sorry to have to inform you that the message returned below could not be delivered to one or more destinations.

For further assistance, please send mail to <postmaster>

If you do so, please include this problem report. You can delete your own text from the message returned below.

Unlucky is duly concerned. Why are those mails being sent to him? Has he a virus (maybe)?

And then the final mail from the ISP, the axe appears to fall. An email arrives that reads like this:

To :unlucky@isp.net

Subject : Account Termination Notice

From :admin@isp.net

You have violated your user agreement by sending out bulk email. Your account will be terminated in 24 hours.

---

[7] The next section is this chapter provides more detailed information on the organizational issues associated with the use and distribution of SSL.

If your account has been hijacked and you have not sent these emails, confirm your account at the following web page:

http://accountverify.isp.net

Enter your verifying information. Your account will not be terminated and a record of the hijacking of your account will be investigated

For further assistance, please send mail to <administrator>

The stress So Unlucky immediately goes to the account verification page, reports the hijacking and exhales with relief

Unfortunately for Unlucky, the web page is a false pointer. Spammers who first sent out multiple emails with Unlucky's address targeted Unlucky, knowing he had received these "bounced" emails. When people complained to Unlucky's ISP, the ISP saw the underlying routing information and knew Unlucky was not spamming. However, Unlucky did not have the same information.

The spammers knew they had targeted Unlucky (along with hundreds of others) and guessed that Unlucky did not know how to read the path of an email. Unlucky has given his personal information to the very people who spammed him.

Similarly a warning that your computer *"has been running slower than usual it may be infected with spyware. To scan your computer, click yes below."* Clicking simply delivers you to the page of the company that sent the heavily streamed ads that slowed your computer.

Beware of solutions that emerge immediately after the problem has been experienced, especially if the solution is to offer up your information. Again, security requires privacy.

Third-Party Assertions of Identity

The browser lock is an example of third party reassurance of the integrity of a website. Traditional providers of credentials for business include the Better Business Bureau and the Consumers Union[8]. Third party assertions of identity and attributes range from cryptographically secure to graphics that are trivial to forge.

There is no simple way for an end user to determine if the third party certification is secure; that is, if the authentication is weak or strong. Third party certification includes established organizations (e.g., Better Business

---

[8] The Consumers Union published Consumer Reports.

Bureau) or Internet-only organizations (e.g., TRUSTe, Verisign). In either case, the third party organization is paid by the Internet entity that is trying to appeal to the customer. While there have been claims of security, even the highly vaunted Verisign security products have been subverted.

With the absence of familiar cues, users are likely to transfer trust by first extending trust to entities that have a real-world counterpart, those that have been recommended to them, or entities that have an established brand reputation. Third party certification, when it works, makes the market more competitive because it allows consumers to make an informed choice to trust previously unknown merchants.

The Secure Sockets Layer (SSL) is the ubiquitous security infrastructure of the Internet. SSL provides confidentiality during browsing by establishing a cryptographically secure connection between two parties (such as a customer and a merchant) that can then be used to conduct commerce transactions. The SSL layer ensures confidentiality, i.e. passwords, credit card numbers, and other sensitive information cannot be easily compromised by third parties through eavesdropping. SSL is excellent at meeting its design goal of preventing eavesdropping. It does *not* function as a reliable identification and credentialing service for web sites. The reason SSL fails in this function is, in part, the economics of the market for certificates.

SSL does not shelter the consumer's information from insecure merchant machines, nor does it prevent the merchant from exploiting the acquired information.

A claimed identity, called "owner's name or alias" in Internet Explorer (IE) documentation is linked to an SSL certificate. In January 2004, the number of trusted roots by default the IE version for Windows XP exceeded one hundred and continued to grow. The listed entities are primarily financial institutions and commercial certificate authorities (CA) but also include a multitude of businesses that have associations with Microsoft, for whom it is convenient to be included as default. Noted cryptographer Matt Blaze has observed that the largest commercial CA, Verisign, protects consumers from anyone who will not give Verisign money.

Thus currently implemented CA's are problematic in multiple dimensions. First, the Internet Explorer default is a broad and fundamental inclusion of commercial entities as trustworthy, yet there has been no interaction by the customer. Indeed even competent and otherwise reliable merchants may have practices strongly disliked by a customer. Second, the CA bears no liability for the behavior of those parties they have certified. The certification only indicates that the CA authenticated the claim of the requestor of a domain name. Most certificates do not have any implications for the business practices of organizations that are associated with the domain names. Therefore, there is a strong and consistent incentive for CA's to certify as many parties as broadly as possible.

Another common form of third party verification is third-party trust seals. Third party seals from organizations such as the Better Business

Bureau, TRUSTe, and Verisign are used to indicate a compliance with specific business practices, fair information practices, as well as verify digital credentials. The seals are especially targeted to new Internet companies that do not have a reputation in the real world, but would still like to establish a relationship with clientele.

Unfortunately, several problems are inherent in the seal solution. First, the seals themselves are digital images that can be easily acquired and displayed by malicious websites, thereby effectively exploiting a customer's trust. Subsequently, once an online merchant has procured a seal, no one attempts to ensure that the merchant continues to comply with all the policies because the burden of such a task would be too great. Third, a certification by a third party will not make a site automatically trustworthy. The certification is only as trustworthy as the certifying party. Finally, the seals only confirm that the merchant complies with a privacy policy. Not only is there no confirmation of the quality of security of the merchants' site, but it is also the case that the site's privacy policy may be exploitive or consist of an assertion of complete rights over customer data.

Figure 2a	*Figure 2b*	*Figure 2c*

Figure 2: Examples of Trust Seals

For example, the TRUSTe seal (Figure 2a) indicates only that the site has a privacy policy and follows it. In many cases, this seal in fact implies an exploitive policy declaring users have no privacy. If the company complied with the Children's On-line Protection Act or with the European Privacy Directive then the company could obtain the seals in 2b or 2c. Of course, any American business is required to comply with the law, so Figure 2b is less than a gold standard. In effect, the most popular seal on the web is as much a warning sign on the state of privacy practice as a reassurance.

An empirical study examined the top web sites based on search rank for a series of common search terms. The author of the study, Ben Edelman, then checked two factors. First, he examined each web site's privacy policy. Second, he left his computer open so that any attempt from the web site to download spyware or malicious code would be detected. He found that those sites with TRUSTe web seals were significantly more likely to download malicious code and to have exploitive privacy policies than those without. So the most common mechanism for identification of web sites as trustworthy is sometimes a warning flag.

Identification must be mutual to be effective. I must be able to authenticate that I am communicating with a bank to confirm in any meaningful way that I am a customer of the bank. The combination of exploitive privacy policies and actual installation of malicious code from certified trusted sites are the perfect complement to the standard of identification that now exist: provide an unverified web site all your information, and you may be able to make a purchase. The current practices require us to prove identity through personal disclosure. It's not the only option, as described in later chapters. It is an option that minimizes security by minimizing privacy. It is prevalent because the alternatives require more investment in customers and technology.

Proving Identity Through Personal Disclosure

Information disclosure systems are those that allow a web-based entity to assert that its behavior is trustworthy, and the user of the site is left with the decision to believe those assertions or not. The assertions that are presented include privacy policies, and the automated evaluation of policies. Information disclosure is distinguished from third party certificates because the site asserts a claim with no centralized or secondary verification.

Privacy policies are assertions of trustworthy behavior by merchants. Privacy policies may be difficult to read, and may vary in subtle ways. The Platform for Privacy Preferences (P3P) was, according to the developers, designed to enable individuals to more easily evaluate and interpret a website's privacy policy.[9] P3P requires a vendor to generate an XML file which describes the information practices of the website; this file can then be automatically read by the web browser and compared with a user's preset preferences. Microsoft incorporated P3P into Internet Explorer 6.0. However, Microsoft's implementation is so limited that P3P primarily functions as a cookie manager.

AT&T created a plug-in for Internet Explorer called the "Privacy Bird" in hopes of encouraging utilization to the full potential of P3P. The Privacy Bird compares the privacy policy of a site with the expressed preferences of the end user. The bird provides simple feedback (e.g., by singing, changing color, issuing cartoon expletives) to end users to enable them to make more informed choices. The Privacy Bird is arguably the most effective user interaction mechanism for evaluating privacy policies to date.

---

[9] Hochheiser, 2002 noted that the substantive result from P3P was the defeat of the proposed privacy rules for online businesses. To the extent that P3P was designed to enhance consumer privacy, it has not obviously succeeded. To the extent it was created by W3C to prevent privacy regulation under the self-regulation argument, it has been a remarkable success.

However, it responds to unsubstantiated claims and there is no mechanism to prevent post-transactional policy change.

The core problem with P3P is that the protocol relies on the vendor to provide an honest and thorough accounting of the information practices on the website, which again forces consumers to place trust in the vendor. The protocol does not have a mechanism for validation of the vendor's claims. So the Privacy Bird may mislead a consumer to trust an objectionable site. Also, in the case of IE 6.0, poor implementation of the user interface counteracted the protocol's attempt to be simple yet informative. The IE 6.0's privacy thermostat used a privacy scale from "low" to "high" yet the differences between the settings are neither immediately apparent nor well-documented.

The automated evaluation of privacy polices may be effective in empowering consumers; however there is no mechanism for feedback or shared experiences in P3P.

Signaling Identities

Internet fraud, enabled by a lack of reliable, trusted sources of information, is a large and growing problem and is based primarily upon the inability of individuals to identify merchants. (FTC, 2004; PEW 2002) The Federal Trade Commission has reported that in 2004, 53% of all fraud complaints were Internet-related (FTC, 2005) with identity theft topping the list with 246,570 complaints, up 15% from the previous year. (FTC, 2005) PEW has noted that 68% of Internet users surveyed were concerned about criminals obtaining their credit card information, while 84% were worried about compromise of other personal information. (PEW, 2002b) The prevalence of fraud makes consumers more suspicious of e-commerce.

As an example consider the phishing attack discussed above. Phishing is difficult to prevent because it preys directly on the absence of contextual signals in trust decisions online. Absent any information other than an email from a self-proclaimed bank, the user must evaluate a website that is nearly identical to the site he or she has used without much consideration. Simultaneously, there is very little that an institution can do to show that it is not a masquerade site. If consumers continue to misplace their trust in the information vacuum, losses will accumulate. If they decide to avoid such risks, then the economy loses a valuable commercial channel.

Another form of attack is web sites that download malicious code, or exploit browser vulnerabilities to create zombies[10]. For example, a study by Microsoft using monkey spider browsers (browsers which spider the web but

---

[10] Zombies are machines that are remotely controlled by malicious parties. These are usually home computers, which are utilized by criminals to phish, send spam, and commit other online crimes.

act like humans) found 752 sites that subverted machines via browser vulnerabilities. (Wang et. al. 2006)

Individuals in fact have been destroyed by information security failures. Currently, in Connecticut in the U.S., a substitute teacher named Julie Amero is under threat of forty years imprisonment for showing students pornography. Told "Do Not Under Any Circumstances Turn Off the Computer," she felt she had no recourse when malware began displaying obscene pictures to the classroom of seventh graders. (Smith, 2006)

In an even more severe case, thirty-four people in the United Kingdom killed themselves after being charged with downloading child pornography based entirely on credit card purchases. Commodore David White killed himself within 24 hours after the charges, after which it was determined that there was no evidence on his own computer, cameras, or memory devices that he had ever downloaded such material. Another killed himself after being declared "innocent"[11] of downloading child pornography. In the two years of the investigation, he had been divorced, denied custody of his children, refused employment, and socially shamed for being a pedophile based upon the records of one computer transaction. (Herbert, 2005) An emergency room doctor, in contrast, cleared his name when the judge declared that credit card records alone, with no pornography on the doctor's machines, was evidence only of credit card fraud. (BBC, 2004).

In the physical realm there are useful visual, geographical and tactile cues that indicate a merchant's professionalism, competence, and even trustworthiness. In e-commerce, parties to a transaction commonly are geographically, temporally, and socially separated.

Consider the illustrations in Figure 3 below. These are both places where one might purchase pearls. Were these markets meters, as opposed to continents, apart there would still be no way to confuse the two.

In economic terms Tiffany's has the higher quality and is able to signal this quality through the construction of an impressive facade, location at a prestigious address, and a highly ordered self-presentation.

In contrast, the signaling in the Ladies' Market indicates high competition, low overhead, and strong downward pressure on prices. In the Hong Kong market, merchants may assure buyers that the pearls are real, perhaps even harvested in Japan. The buyer may be assured that the low prices are a result of once-in-a-lifetime opportunity, and that the buyer should not hesitate at this rare chance at owning such high quality pearls. The overall context of the transaction provides information useful in evaluating these claims.

---

[11] The judge noted that the court could only declare him, "not guilty", but that he would rather that it be clear in this case the accused had been completely exonerated.

Ladies' Jewelry Market, Hong Kong   Entry to Tiffany's

Figure 3: Shopping Offline Provides Context

Online these virtual sites would be distinguished only by the web site design, domain name, and corresponding SSL certificates. Imagine one of the merchants in the Hong Kong were named Tifanny. In February 2006, the domain name Tifanny.net is available for tens of dollars. Even with the cryptographic centralized provision of SSL certificates as described above, would be possible. In contrast, brick and mortar businesses can invest in physical infrastructure and trusted physical addresses to send signals about their level of prestige, customer service and reliability. For example, a business on the fiftieth block of Fifth Avenue (arguably the most expensive real estate in New York and thus America) has invested more in its location than a business in the local mall that has in turn invested more than a roadside stall. The increased investment provides an indicator of past success and potential loss in the case of criminal action. Information on such investment is far less available on the Internet. The domain "tifany.us" is available in 2007, but creating an equally believable offline version of Tiffany's requires far more investment.

To emphasize the point, compare the following images: Sun Trust Bank and an organized crime outlet.

One site provides electronic banking for customers of Sun Trust Bank. The other is a computer in Columbia University that was controlled at the moment of that screen shot by a criminal entity (quite possibly on another continent). There is no mechanism for the bank to signal to the virtual customer its investment and thus its quality and authenticity. Any signaling is limited to the form of mass-produced easily copied images (e.g., TRUSTe or BBB trust seals) or SSL certificates.

Only the SSL icon indicates that the individual is in a low trust environment, because in this case the phisher has purchased a domain name that does not provide distinguishing information. In economic terms, of the ease of falsification is enabled because there are no signals.

Recall that even SSL certificates can be falsified enough to fool humans into trusting behavior and provision of identity information. Falsification of cues is far, far easier than from breaking cryptographic security. Recall the examples above, of masquerades with confusing domain names (as is the case here with checking-suntrust.com) and SSL-enabled phishing.

Figure 4: Shopping Without Context

Security experts immediately recognize the false site. Many users also recognize the false site, based on its domain name and the lack of the icon indicating a SSL certificate.

Identity systems can be centralized or based upon social networks. (See Chapter 13 for more detail on social networks and reputations.) No identification can prevent confusion; and thus no system can prevent every fraud. However, targeted, user-centered systems could prevent the masquerade attacks discussed here by identifying the merchant or bank to the customer. Privacy-enhancing identification systems could prevent the phishing attacks described here from enabling identity theft. Privacy-enhancing identity thefts prevent attacks that can be leveraged into cascading failures of identification by limiting information use, and preventing re-use of information. Anonymous credentials that can empower consumers to protect privacy while improving authentication are described in Chapter 10.

6.   Secrecy, Privacy, Identity

Phishing attacks are so profitable because they enable cascading failures. Online identity systems that are built upon concepts of papers and identification enable these cascading failures in part because such systems do not protect privacy.

Privacy, confidence and trust are about the distribution of power. Privacy offers me the ability to act freely, as a citizen, in my own home without my government or employer watching me. Privacy offers me the power to protect myself. Privacy also allows me to use illegal drugs or commit acts of violence in my home, despite government prohibition and employer chagrin. Privacy can enable harming others.

Privacy is violated only when identifying information is associated with other data. There are no privacy issues with anonymous grocery cards, not because with work and determination the shopper cannot be identified. There are not privacy concerns because the work required is so much higher than the value of the identifying information. There are not privacy concerns in inventory or tracking purchase correlations (e.g., giving out cat litter coupons upon the purchase of cat food). Privacy is only an issue when there is identity in a record, or when identity can be easily extracted from the record.

Yet privacy is double-edged sword. One person's privacy can reduce another person's autonomy. A classic use of privacy to control is described in "The Unwanted Gaze" where Rosen discusses the dual problems of privacy in sexual harassment. Sexual harassment investigations allow for intrusive investigations, against both claimants and those charged. Yet the lack of sexual harassment laws created a sphere of privacy that was used for abuse of power. The pundit O'Reilly had his secret sexual fantasies exposed when his producer played the tapes of his obscene phone calls. Powerful men demanded women's bodies for the women to keep their jobs. Exploitation of this type, called quid pro quo, is now not only illegal but widely socially condemned. Bragging about sleeping with a secretary is as contemptible as driving drunk – another change in social mores based on the balance between individual autonomy and the good of others. Yet the practices of exploitive sex in the workplace was an element of the existence of privacy, just like domestic violence and child abuse. The relationship between my privacy and your security is complex.

Indeed it was the sanctity of the family that prevented child abuse laws to the point where the first successful child abuse prosecution was under laws against cruelty to animals. (In 1874 animals were legally protected but children were not. In the case of the horribly abused Mary Ellen McCormack, the first successful child abuse prosecution in the United States, the judge depended on cruelty to animal laws to sentence the mother to 1 year of prison. The next year the New York Society for the Prevention of Cruelty to Children was founded based on the model of the NY Society for the Prevention of Cruelty to Animals.) Child abuse laws were seen as invasions into the privacy of the family. Privacy can be the opposite of accountability. For example, Rosen defends a concept of privacy that is brutal. A perfectly private world risks being one where violence is never investigated, where identities can be snuffed out. Privacy that prevents a person from bearing witness to her own experiences does not create freedom. But privacy that makes every interaction recorded merchandise creates its own threats to freedom.

This balance in autonomy, the downside to privacy is widely heralded and embraced in discussions about security. No doubt children, though lacking full legal protection until age eighteen, are better off with child abuse laws than without them. No doubt the family that is wrongly accused might disagree, so the ability to accuse and investigate is tightly constrained.

Yet the balance between security and privacy is not so absolute. A lack of privacy can weaken security. Privacy cuts both ways in terms of security.

A lack of privacy can mean no autonomy. A life lived under surveillance is not a free life.

A lack of secrecy can mean a lack of security. Without privacy there is no secrecy. When all is exposed there are no secrets. Identity theft, phishing, and much computer crime, is enabled because there is no secrecy for the supposed private information. Indeed, an Illinois Appellate court has determined that sharing information, including names, addresses, and social security is not an invasion of privacy. The basis for the decision that cell phone companies can use subscriber information was that none of information shared (including - names, cell phone numbers, billing addresses, and social security numbers) were private facts. In this case, no privacy means no security. (Busse v. Motorola, Inc., 2004 Ill. App. LEXIS 738 (1st Dist. June 22, 2004))

Yet unlike secrecy (we all agree on the nature of a secret) there is great divide in people's perceptions of privacy. Age, gender, employment, and generally the person's place in the overall hierarchy effect their beliefs about the value and nature of privacy (Wilfords, 2002). Individual politics and belief systems alter our conceptions of privacy – a libertarian and a liberal have different views about government limits on business use of personal data. Yet both have the same understanding (albeit possibly different opinions) about classified or secret data.

The loss of privacy in the cases where security is decreased is deeply intertwined with identity and identity management.

On the surface, there is a seemingly inherent tradeoff between identity and privacy. Privacy-enhancing identity management is not an oxymoron. Privacy and ubiquitous ID systems can, together, serve to enhance individual autonomy. Of course, there is a conflict between the designer's desire to have information to make optimal use of the system and the subject's right to privacy, that is, their control of information about themselves. Yet carefully selecting information and deciding in the design stage who will have access to and control of information can enhance functionality while protecting privacy.

Making privacy function in identity design requires understanding the various dimensions of privacy. The technology implemented by a designer can vary based on the designers' conception of privacy (e.g., Phillips, 2004; Camp & Osorio, 2003). Thus in the following chapter I examine different conceptions of privacy, from Constitutional law to technical practice.

Laws of Identity

The debate on privacy in terms of identity was greatly enhanced by the creation and support by Microsoft of the "laws of identity". Obviously these are not laws, they are too vague and guarantee nothing. Yet they provide an excellent framework for considering identity systems. Are these the laws that should be adopted?

User-centric identity is a grand phrase. Yet can be a disaster. It depends on the details. Like use of SSNs user-centric identity, users can be effectively forced to consent. In the worst case user-centric identity simply extends the reach of personal data. Within a federated identity, there is a limit to the federation, so personal information flow is limited to the federation. User-centric identity can result in accelerated transmission of personal data as every party requires information from the user to interact.

User control and consent brings up the question of consent. In theory, we have all consented to the current state of data publicity. By interacting with companies that sell data to data resellers we consent to the use of our data. By providing information for a loan, we provide information for ChoicePoint to fax to identity thieves (upon valid payment). Consent has proven woefully inadequate thus far for the protection of authenticating and identifying information.

Minimal disclosure for a defined use is a foundation of privacy. In fact, few consent to resell of data. Yet when the choice is to sign the mortgage, close the loan and move or to pursue a fruitless search of banks for a reasonably privacy policy, we must consent. Minimal disclosure for defined purpose would imply that our identifying information would be provided only to obtain a mortgage, not to generate additional business in data resale for the lender.

Justifiable use is as difficult as consent. Marginal decreased use for the data collector justifies, for the collector, the request for data. After the data are all collected, profit inherently justifies resale.

Directional identity implies that identity can be proven to one party, so that the authenticating party cannot simply sell the information to others who may or may not be interested in various masquerade attacks.

The first four are privacy principles, the others are about good design practices.

Pluralism of operators and technologies is the final "identity law." This implies that no one party can own identity. In fact, forcing discrete agencies to create their own identities implies that each is responsible for that identifier. If the movie rental agency had to create its own records, the company might require a membership fee. However, the fee could be returned with consistent responsible behavior. Similarly, telephone companies require either a (refundable) deposit or a Social Security Number with the corresponding record.

Other identity requirements can be added. For example, user control as implied above, is meaningless without user empowerment. To the extent that these are "laws" then they should be instantiated in the technology and as difficult to violate as gravity. Anonymous credentials would fulfill the requirements of consent, exposure and disclosure in a technical mechanism. Yet this requires investment in a new infrastructure.

Privacy as Spatial

Doors exist to be as much to be shut as to be open. Doors, walls, structures, and neighborhoods create boundaries both in terms of appropriate behavior and trust. Boundaries both reinforce and support self defined choices and identities. Neighbors are trusted not only because of the self-sorting of modern neighborhoods but also because the cost of a dispute is so high.

Privacy in computing is often conceived of as an issue of boundaries. (Jaing, 2002; Langheinrich, 2002; Boyle, 2003; Geraci, 2004) Many technology designers have adopted a concept of contested social spaces as articulated in the concept of privacy as process. (Altman, 1975) Contested social spaces are spaces where you are not in secret but may or may not be identified. For example, in a train station or in the mall you may identify yourself for payment. There is a record created of the purchase that places you in one location. Or perhaps you may pay cash. There is no formal record of identification for being in that place. However, the place is not private in the sense that there are social behaviors that are inappropriate in these clearly public places.

Social spaces are now anonymous by choice of the designers or owners. Video systems are widely used. Video systems can be linked to face recognition. More likely, credit cards and identification will become wireless, so the mall or street or train station can continuously check to see who is present. The population of the mall could readily offer the specials, the pricing, and the sales especially to the extent that advertisements and pricing information is provided electronically. There is an incentive for identification of who is in the mall.

The boundary concept strongly parallels the early work on regulation of speech on the Internet, in which legal and policy scholars disputed the nature of cyberspaces.[12] (Naughton, 1992) (Sunstein, 1995) In both digital speech and digital privacy, spatial metaphors were adopted because of the potential power of the heuristic. Spatial metaphors enabled the classification of contests with historical conflicts of speech. Spatial metaphors offer great subtlety. Like the speech debate, the spatial privacy discourse has integrated issues of social, natural and temporal spaces. (Langheinrich, 2002) Being at the mall at midnight when it is closed is quite distinct from being there at 8pm when it is open.

The difference between virtual and physical spaces is determined by the nature of the boundaries that divide them. Virtual boundaries are distinct in three dimensions: simultaneity, permeability and exclusivity. (Camp & Chien, 2001) Simultaneity refers to the ability of a person to be two places at once: at work and at the mall. The mall might attempt to determine who is there. Should it be able to sell the information of who is at the mall to employers, in order to determine who is taking an extended lunch break December 22? What of the case when you are shopping at work?

Suzie,

Given that Joey has been having trouble in school I thought I might purchase the phonics package. What do you think of this resource?

http://www.dyslexia-parent.com/course.html

thanks,

Lucy

In this case the law argues that the business needs only to have a business need to read the email. However, sitting at the desk the individual is experiencing an interaction in multiple dimensions. Sitting at work, even on break, the person is an employee. Sending an email the person is both parent (to Suzie) and grandparent (to Joey). Examining the task and asking another person, the person is a consumer. Lucy identifies herself to the computer at work to access her web mail. She identifies herself to her web-based personal email provider via a password. She identifies herself to the recipient of the question by her originating email address. Lucy is in multiple spaces because the virtual spaces of the web-based email, the store, and the workplace are

---

[12] This debate was settled when Internet Service Providers obtained a Safe Harbor provision in the Digital Millennium Copyright Act that delineated appropriate ISP behavior with regards to copyright (a most troublesome modern speech/property conflict) and expression.

simultaneous. The employer may use application-level proxies. In this case the employer has every identifier. Of course, employers are not monolithic organizations but are entities made of human beings. Should the IT workers (somewhere on the globe) have access to all the identifiers and communications created by the complex interaction? In a physical space, the existence of boundaries allows for the separation of identifiers. The existence of multiple simultaneous virtual spaces can concentrate risk. A criminal IT support party can obtain all Lucky's identifiers – perhaps even her credit card depending on the operation of the firewall should Lucy choose to purchase the Multi-Modal learning package under consideration.

Permeability is the capacity of ICTs to make spatial, organizational or functional barriers more powerful, less powerful, or even invisible. The permeability of the work/home barrier is most clearly illustrated with telecommuting. Barriers can be so permeable as to be transversed without the knowledge of the person putatively moving across the boundary. For example, moving from a conference site to the payment processor or from a web site to an affiliate is intended to be seamless. Similarly some blogs (a notably annoying feature dropped by e-commerce sites) keep a reader framed so that the reader cannot easily escape one blog into another. In one case the user crosses boundaries and experiences simultaneity, and in the other the user attempts to cross boundaries and is constrained by invisible ties. In case, identities and authentication information crosses boundaries and risk can be multiplied.

Exclusivity, in contrast, is the ability of ICTs to create spaces that are impermeable, or even imperceptible, to others. Intranets may offer exclusive access through a variety of access control mechanisms, and the creation of databases that are invisible to the subjects clearly illustrates the capacity for exclusivity.

In the physical sphere, the walled private developments offer an excellent example of exclusivity, yet it is not possible to make physical spaces so exclusive as to be invisible. In digital spaces discovery of places one is not allowed to view is itself problematic. Technologies redefine the nature of space, and digital networked technologies alter the nature of boundaries. (Shapiro, 1998)

Exclusivity is possible for identities. Secure hardware, encrypted interactions, and protection of authentication information allows for exclusive identification. Exclusivity means that one lost identifier does not cause a cascading effect. For example, loss of a gym locker combination does not create a lack of security elsewhere. The locker is exclusive so that accessing the locker does not allow access into the home. In the virtual realm, loss of control of a computer desktop will allow access to other dimensions. Loss of information used for cross-domain authentication (e.g., Social Security Numbers) creates systematic failures. In the virtual world it is if whenever a locker is broke, one's keys and wallet are by definition in that locker at that movement. Physical exclusivity implicitly provides failure isolation. Virtual exclusivity can do the same.

Communities online are often imagined communities. For example, the Face Book is considered an extension of the campus life. Students conceive of this as a safe place that is not going to be part of life after they graduate.

The share of users of high sensitivity to partner or sexual orientation who claim to be concerned about sexuality is nearly three-quarters. Yet fully half of these have posted that information on Face Book. Only one in five realizes that anyone can search the data. 85% do not believe that The Face Book will collect information from other sources. Three quarters do not believe the Face Book will give away information. Yet the privacy policy is clear about resale and release of information.

Almost 70% suggest that *others* are putting themselves at risk when those others post behavioral information. Yet when asked why they put information up, the majority of users identify expressing themselves as having fun.

The students are imagining boundaries that do not exist. The students live in an imagined community. They believe the virtual information space is exclusive. The privacy policy is clear about compilation and resale of information. But the image of a virtual space is so strong, that they trust information they declare that they would not share.

Data Protection

Due to the complexity of the problem of privacy and ever increasing data flows, the European Union, Canada, and Australia have adopted data protection regimes. The Code of Fair Information Practice is the foundation of the dominant data protection regimes. The Code (and the related data protection requirements) has as its core *transparency, consent, and correction*. In terms of privacy, these are generally seen as a reasonable minimum. Transparency requires that no data compilation be secret.

Consent can be problematic even when the installation is clearly visible. Informed consent implies an understanding of the underlying sensor technology and the data that can be compiled. Consent includes not only awareness of the existence of data in sorted form, but also consent to the various uses of that data. Consent requires that data can be deleted or corrected when desired by the subject.

Data protection regimes have the advantage of mitigating the complex dimensions of privacy. In contrast, the multi-level jurisdictional approach has the advantage of illuminating the sometimes competing dimensions of privacy.

Data protection defines some data as inalienable (e.g., sexual orientation) and other data as subject to contract (e.g., name, address, date and amount of a purchase). The clean, carefully drawn lines about particular data elements in data protection are inadequate for the continuous data flow with probabilistic potential to detail all factors of our lives.

Data protection differs from identity principles. But data protection can limit the abuse and construction of identity. For example, Canadian identity principles require that identifiers justify the use of identity. Unfortunately, as long as all payment mechanisms are linked to identity, provision of easily stolen information is required for commerce. However, data protection also requires that there be a reason for identity information. Also, the resale of identifying information is not allowed under data protection requirements.

Autonomy

Autonomy has traditionally been a central concern of legal scholars in privacy. In the literature of democracy, privacy is autonomy. Privacy as a Human Right under the UN Universal Declaration of Human Rights is based on the freedom to act without the fear of surveillance. Surveillance can result in targeted retaliation. Similarly, the European Data protection regime recognizes informational autonomy by declaring that there are data that cannot be collected except under highly constrained circumstances, for example data on sexual preference. Legal monographs on privacy tend often focus exclusively on the autonomy concept of privacy (e.g., Alderman and Kennedy, 1995).

Privacy is a form of autonomy because a person under surveillance is not free. In the United States, Constitutional definitions of privacy are based on autonomy, not seclusion. These decisions have instituted both sexual autonomy and, in the case of postal mail and library records, a tradition of information autonomy under the law.

This concept of information autonomy was altered under the USA PATRIOT Act but still remains central in American jurisprudence.

Autonomy is more than agency. Autonomy is the ability to act without threat of retaliation and thus refers to freedom of action and patterns of actions that are not mitigated by surveillance. In NAACP v. Alabama, the opinion sums up the requirement for autonomy for a legal regime, "a government purpose to control or prevent activities constitutionally subject to regulation may not be achieved by means which sweep unnecessarily broadly and thereby invade the area of protected freedoms." A technical modification may be "a technological purpose to control or prevent activities subject to surveillance may not be achieved by means which sweep unnecessarily broadly and thereby invade the area of preferred freedoms."

Autonomy as privacy became part of the popular discourse in the United States in 1965 because of two decisions by the Supreme Court that year. In the first, a unanimous Court struck down the Congressional statutory authorization of the Post Office to detain mail the USPS determined to be "communist political propaganda" and to release that mail only after the addressee notified the USPS in writing that he or she wanted that specific information. (Lamont v. Postmaster General) Later the Court reviewed an arrest of a Director of Planned Parenthood who was providing contraception and information about contraception to a married couple. The law prohibiting such communication was abolished in a split court with the decision Griswold v. Connecticut. These two decisions form the underpinning of the right to privacy. Both are decisions based on the availability of information. Of course the later decision Roe v. Wade, which secured the right to legal abortion, is the privacy law most prevalent in the American mind.

Privacy as autonomy, privacy as a human right, is inalienable. Only the concept of privacy as autonomy provides the theoretical underpinning for individuals' interest in data about themselves absent quantified harm. Recognizing that individuals have interests in data that extends beyond immediate harm is recognition of the right to privacy as autonomy.

In technical systems, privacy as autonomy is usually implemented as strong anonymity. Users who seek autonomy in a particular dimension will seek data deletion, anonymity or obfuscation.

In addition to the very real threats of crime and abuse of power, privacy is also trumped by speech in the United States. The First Amendment is absolute, "Congress shall make no law respecting an establishment of religion, or prohibiting the free exercise thereof; or abridging the freedom of speech, or of the press; or the right of the people peaceably to assemble, and to petition the Government for a redress of grievances." "No law" is taken by many to mean "no law". In contrast, privacy has no such absolute protection.

Property

Privacy in the United States is a subject of both civil (that is state law) as well as federal Constitutional law. Thus privacy is also a tort (or rather a set for four torts that need not be specified here) in the United States. Privacy as a tort defines privacy as essentially commercial, a wrong that can be set right by payment.

Privacy can yield economic advantage to select stakeholders. (Bloustein, 1968; Mell, 1996) For example, data that provides demographic information and thus enables price discrimination can violate this dimension of privacy.

User behavior with respect to personal information, valuation of protection of information, and characterization of data types with respect to the subject identification are all topics of active economics research. (Camp & Lewis, 2004)

The objection to privacy as property is that property rights are alienable. Under the property paradigm all subject interests in property are lost at the transaction. A data subject has no more right to limit secondary use of data than a seller of a home has a right to return and paint the kitchen after the closing. (Samuelson, 2000)

In either case, the data are economically valuable and thus centralized authorities will have economic incentives to share those data. (Odlyzko, 2004) Users who see data as property will want payment for data. Alternatively, users may seek deniable pseudonyms in order to avoid future price discrimination or to prevent complete loss of control over personally identifiable data.

Sign on the Virtual Line

> I reach out my hand and push the browser button down. In response, the task bar slowly fills from left to right. I have digitally signed a document.

> I sign my name across the small black screen to authenticate my credit purchase. I have created a digitized record of my signature.

> My fax is signed. I send it to authorize my purchase. I have sent a signature that was physical, digitized and then printed into an analog physical form.

Each of these actions has very different implications in terms of my own risk, and the ability of others to misuse the information sent to spend my money, or otherwise pretend to be me to obtain payment authorization.

The last is the easiest to understand and the only case where there is a true signature. But why would my handwriting be adequate to authorize a monetary transaction? I simply claim to be me and send a scrap of paper. Here is my handwriting, and it represents me. Why is sending a fax (possibly from a fax machine that can be accessed for a small cash payment) superior to making the same claim of identity over the phone? In part, this is because there are legal and organizational mechanisms that allow that signature to be verifiable later for dispute resolution.

Digital signatures or cryptographic signatures use the science of hiding information. The hiding of information using codes has long been the purview of government and high finance. Codes were not always mathematical. Caesar implemented one of the oldest recorded tricks for hiding information. He wanted to send a message through hostile territory via a messenger. But the messenger might be captured and killed or even subject to torture to obtain any secret message. Thus Caesar had to send a message that could not be read by the messenger or any person who intercepted the messenger. Having something unreadable by the messenger was simple; any illiterate slave would fill that condition. However, any slave would be unlikely to endure torment in order to protect an owner's secrets. In this case the solution was to write the message on the slave's head with strong ink and then, after having grown back his hair, the slave was sent with the message to the recipient. ("The Codebreakers" by Kahn is the canonical history of cryptography, and the source of this tale and other.)

Despite the fact that this approach is wildly inappropriate today, it achieves some of the same goals that mathematical cryptography does today. First, the bearer of the message cannot read the message. Neither the Roman slave nor the modern ISP is a reliable agent of the interest of the sender. In technical terms the message was *confidential*.

However, there is an effective attack against both systems. If the slave cooperates with any party intercepting the slave then the message may be read. That is, the slave may simply tell the messenger how to access the secret ("It's under my hair.") Then, the slave's head is shaved and voila! The attacker has the message. The slave is literally the man in the middle, and his cooperation can subvert security.

Similarly there are man-in-the-middle attacks online. In this case, the man-in-the-middle is the attacker and the transmitter of messages. Online, the man-in-the-middle masquerades as both parties, each to the other. The man-in-the-middle pretends to be the bank to the customer, and the customer to the bank. The man-in-the-middle sets up a web site that appears to be the bank site to the customer. The customer enters authenticating information: password, account number, or whatever else is needed. The man-in-the-middles sends this to the bank, and confirms to the customer that the information is correct. The man-in-the-middle then may even accurately perform actions on behalf of the user while the user is logged on. However, the man-in-the-middle will not log off and will certainly abuse the account information provided.

If the slave showed up with head shaved (unlikely if he were rewarded for cooperation, impossible if he were killed) then the recipient would know there was interference. In technical terms this means a loss of confidentiality is detectable. Thus writing on the head of person provides a secure communication system that *is tamper evident*. That means you can tell if the message had been altered or accessed without authorization. There is a nice feature of the shorn slave for the ancient royal correspondents. That is an advantage to writing on a slave as opposed to writing on the Internet – any loss of confidentiality is more easily detected in the head-writing case. However, the recipient may not know to expect a message. Caesar's representative, like the banking customer today, sits unaware while the cost of the lost message is amplified by use and time. In the case of digital information there is no readily available method to know if someone has seen the hidden information.

Both security mechanisms (hair and cryptography) share at least one weakness in that it is (relatively) time consuming. Cryptographic signatures time to sending messages because they are processing intensive. In this case the time is microseconds added to nanoseconds, not weeks added to days.

Sadly there is a correspondence between modern security and the hygiene of ancient Rome that found hair-washing so unimportant. The slave may bring more than the message. The slave might arrive ill, bearing viruses and germs with the gift of information. Similarly secure systems in computers can be subverted and do more harm than good, particularly if subverted. Messages received may bear more than the content.

7. Security and Privacy as Market Failures

Most software is sold as is, according to the end user licensing agreement. This means that the software is released with bugs, known and unknown. There is tremendous market pressure to push software out the door. Money flows in as soon as the software is written. Being first may mean market dominance.

The resulting software, with errors, may need to be repaired regularly. Indeed, one Tuesday a month for the life of Windows XP Microsoft released patches to address failures in the software. This is software that runs critical systems, and that had been on the market for years.

In part this is because the information economy is relatively new. Code is complex. Even line by line examination of code cannot detect every possible security failure. Some bugs, i.e. vulnerabilities, are a result of interaction between programs. The errors emerge in complex unforeseen ways, as the miracle substance DDT resulted in poisoned birds as well as dead bugs. Some errors emerge not for interaction, but only from unique states in the program. There are bugs that occur only when tens of conditions are simultaneously met, so that they could not be detected even in the most rigorous testing.

The result is that the individual who does not keep his or her machine secure by patching every month is at risk. However, every machine that is not patched creates risks for everyone connected to the network. Like the industrial facilities and home toxins that poisoned communities in the first half of the twentieth century; software vulnerabilities and unpatched home machines poison the network and the information on which virtual life depends.

In formal terms, lack of security can be seen as a particular kind of market failure, an externality. (Camp & Wolfram, 2001) Computer security failures cause downtime and costs to the people other than the ones who either create or do not mitigate these failures. At the most obvious, stolen information enables identity theft. But at a more subtle level, the Internet is a network of trust.

Three common ways in which lack of security on one system harms another are shared trust, increased resources, and the ability for the attacker to confuse the trail. Shared trust is a problem when a system is trusted by another, so the subversion of one machine allows the subversion of another. (For example, when passwords for one machine are kept on another). The use of cookies to save authentication information has made this practice extremely common.

The second issue, increased resources, refers to the fact that attackers can increase resources for attacks by subverting multiple machines. This is most obviously useful in brute force attacks, for example in decryption or in a denial of service attack. Using multiple machines makes a denial of service attack easier to implement, since such attacks may depend on overwhelming the target machine.

Third, subverting multiple machines makes it difficult to trace an attack from its source. When taking a circuitous route an attacker can hide his or her tracks in the adulterated log files of multiple machines. Clearly this allows the attacker to remain hidden from law enforcement and continue to launch attacks. The last two points suggest that costs to hackers fall with the number of machines (and so the difference between the benefits of hacking and the costs increases), similar to the way in which benefits to phone users increase with the number of other phones on the network.

A fourth point is the indirect effect security breaches have on users' willingness to transact over the network. For instance, consumers may be less willing to use the Internet for e-commerce if they hear of incidents of credit card theft. This is a rational response if there is no way for consumers to distinguish security levels of different sites.

Because security is an externality the pricing of software and hardware does not reflect the possibility of and the extent of the damages from security failures associated with the item.

Externalities and public goods are often discussed as if they are the same. They are two similar categories of market failures. A common example of a public good is national security, and it might be tempting to think of the analogies between national security and computer security. National security, and public goods in general, are generally single, indivisible goods. A pure public good is something which is both non-rival (my use of it doesn't affect yours) and non-excludable (once the good is produced, it is hard to exclude people from using it).

Computer security, by comparison, is the sum of a number of individual firms' or peoples' decisions. It is important to distinguish computer security from national security (i.e. externalities from public goods) because the solutions to public goods problem and to externalities differ. The government usually handles the production of public goods, whereas there are a number of examples where simple interventions by the government have created a more efficient private market such that trades between private economic parties better reflect the presence of externalities.

Identity management systems may be a public good. For identity management systems to work they either need to be dedicated to a specific use, or usable by all. If one person can subvert an identity management system, then everyone is at risk for subversion.

SoBig, a virus hat made a splash, is an exemplar of security as an externality. SoBig was motivated by the ability to subvert the computers of naive end users in order to implement fraud through phishing and spam. The creator of SoBig has not been detected by law enforcement. In fact, the lack of consideration of agency in computer crime laws creates criminal liability

Camp 75

for those with computers subverted by SoBig as they are, in fact, spamming, phishing or implementing DoS attacks from their own home machines.

Such an attack had been previously identified as a theoretical possibility the year before it occurred in the First Workshop on the Economics of Computer Security. But it became widely known after SoBig.

The model of computer attacks as infection does not apply because the large financial motivation for subverting identity systems is not addressed. The model of computer crime as warfare fails in the SoBig example because the virus subverts but does not destroy.

In this case the assets are the availability of the network. There are providers who assist in preventing denial of service attacks and targeted assaults. For example, when Microsoft came under attack from the MyDoom worm, the company had an agreement with the Linux-based Akamai to provide content in the case of such an attack. However, few organizations will face a denial of service attack and those that do cannot call on content servers for assistance.

In this case the need is to protect assets and the threats are downtime and loss of confidentiality. Threat mitigation includes making internal billing for security prevention such that the externalities are addressed. For example, if every department is charged for spending time patching their computers, then departments will not want to address the constant stream of patches for Microsoft products.

Every first Tuesday of the month Microsoft issues a set of patches. These may be simply a wish list for Microsoft, containing repairs for functionality bugs that might have been fixed before shipping given no market pressures. It may contain an update to the Digital Rights Management systems that will prevent the computers' owner from controlling music or videos on the machine. In fact, some Microsoft patches have obtained code that defeats other code interoperability in order to increase the relative desirability of Microsoft's competing products. Microsoft patching is time-consuming and not always in the best interest of the user. Thus requiring departments and individuals to invest in this patching is irrational, in the most complimentary terms.

If departments are provided free patching support, and charged based on the vulnerabilities of the network then the pricing reflects the externality. The new risk for changing this accounting system is that it creates incentives for managers to spend too much time looking for vulnerabilities and not enough time on other sources of internal risk. However, in an organization no doubt managers have other responsibilities.

For the individual, the result is push patching and automated zombie repair. Push patching means that the patch is "pushed" into a machine from Microsoft. This places much of the cost of patching onto Microsoft. Microsoft has to track the machines that are registered, check their status, and assure compliance. Starting with XP and continuing with Vista Microsoft also detects and removes known zombie code from home users' machines.

Economics of Security

Why, given the resources and programmers of Microsoft, would the company release code with vulnerabilities, resulting in the creation of a market of zombies? Microsoft is among the great winners of the computer and network revolution. If there were any company that wants to ensure ever-more adoption of broadband and high-speed machines at the home and the office it would be Microsoft. And why don't individuals secure their own machines? Why do we endlessly spam ourselves?

The reason most individuals do not secure their own machines is that security is invisible, complicated and the value is partially recovered by others. While we may spam ourselves as a nation of people with insecure machines, one person is unlikely to knowingly receive a spam from his or her own home machines.

Security is invisible. The value of a clean and secure machine may be as high as the value of a machine with a zombie network. In fact, once recruited into a zombie network there are benefits. Owners of networks of zombies (botnets) take care of their machines. Criminal owners patch the machines to ensure that these resources are not stolen from the original thief. Zombies run processes in polite modes, so the physical owner does not notice the load on the machine. Since it is prohibitively expensive to obtain reliable patching at a reasonable cost from a legal service, being part of a high quality botnet is not a bad deal for the individual home user. Of course, if the criminal controlling the machine installs a keylogger, then the transaction is a very bad one for the home owner.

Those attacks that undermine individual use result in more investment against the invisible threat of botnets. Anti spyware and virus technologies are found on far more machines than up-to-date patches.

Beyond downloading freely available firewalls and anti-spyware code, security is complex. Patching is time-consuming and complex. The result, staying out of a botnet, is of limited value. Indeed, sometime patches contain undesirable code, such as anti-competitive code that disables competing products under the guise of digital rights management.

Wireless routers can be plugged in, and work out of the box. These open routers have positive social value when they are used to share Internet access in a community. Of course, the open bandwidth also can have negative results. Individuals who use resources that others have provided such that the resources remain available to the owners are called free riders. As long as the free riders are polite, not downloading massive content and disconnecting when the connection becomes lower, open networks are valuable to everyone.

Yet when free riders are not polite, or even malicious, the owner of the system has significant risks. Those risks are not apparent. Frankly, the possible risks appear unbelievable until they occur. The teacher in Connecticut, who faces up to forty years in prison because malware caused pornography to pop up on the screen, since the firewall subscription was not renewed, can now define firewalls. Yet this twenty-something teacher never heard of firewalls until one particular failure effectively ended her career. The tens of people in the United Kingdom who killed themselves rather than face prosecution for purchasing child pornography on-line did not all live to see their names cleared. The solicitors of child pornography utilized identity and credit card thefts to their detection and punishment for their crimes. Similarly, the home user who decides to share his or her wireless network, perhaps believing it safe out of the box, likely does not know MAC addressing* or encryption options. Free riders can download unlicensed copies of copyrighted material, launch criminal attacks, connect long enough to command a botnet, or even download that most prohibited material, child pornography. Because the security is complex does not mean it is not necessary.

When the default settings for the administrator account are not changed, wireless routers can distort the network view. At attacker can program a router to provide incorrect information; for example, giving those who use the router a fake page for the eBay login or for any known banking URL. Providing an incorrect network address for a correct URL is called pharming, a derivative of phishing. There is no current installed or available technology to prevent pharming. At Indiana University, there are projects working on comparing the browser's history so that if a site shows up at a radically new IP address the browser will be notified. An expansion of that project will compare the certificate presented by a site at one time with past certificate presentations, again identifying pharming at the user level. But these technologies are works in progress, not fully fledged products.

Because of the problems of invisibility and complexity, security does not follow classical economics. Rational economics would argue that as risk goes up, so does investment in security. Also, as the education and capacity of the user increases at least in theory the personal effort, i.e. the individual cost, to secure a router decreases. Reading complex instructions is easier, or lower cost, to a more educated individual. Similarly, increased wealth means increased risk exposure. Just as the wealthy are more likely to purchase risk-appropriate insurance, so rational economics would argue that the wealthy would be more likely to secure a wireless router. Loss of reputation and loss of income are greater monetary risks with more wealth.

Clearly exposure to criminals increases risk. Arguably, exposure to potential criminals increases risk. Assuming that every person is equally likely to be a criminal, those living in higher density locations face more risks.

---

* MAC addresses are machine addresses. Wireless routers allow their owners to list the set of computers that can connect, based on the unique addresses of these machines. This is not fool-proof. A machine can be programmed to misrepresent its MAC address, just like a person can lie about her own name. When combined with over-the-wire encryption,

In high-density locations, there is also the opportunity to free ride outside of public view.

The economic argument suggests that wealth, education and housing density would increase likelihood of use of security. A study of more than three thousand home routers found none of these factors to make a discernable difference. (Hottell, 2007) In fact, the only factor that was significant in home router encryption use was the ease of use of the security features of the routers. Ease of use includes both the usability (e.g., is there a security wizard?) and defaults (does encryption come on immediately?).

Economics of Privacy

Monitoring and logging user actions are often seen as solutions to a generic security problem. However, security is best used when based on a clear threat model, and an understanding of the dynamics of security in society. Beyond the economic model, there are other conceptual models of security that can assist in understanding the complex technical, organizational, and legal interactions that have created identity theft.

Using a simple model from automobiles, is LoJack worth the investment? Yes, it prevents theft and solves a real problem. In addition it creates a positive externality, which is when Lojack is in use by some people car thefts go down for an entire neighborhood. What about car alarms? They do make noise. However, they are easily disabled and have not been shown to prevent auto theft. Car alarms also create a negative externality. They make neighborhoods less pleasant and decrease social capital. Privacy choices mechanisms are similarly complex.

Unlike the distinction between car alarms and silence, distinguishing between high privacy and low privacy domains can be very difficult. In economic terms, there are no reliable signals. In economics, signals are difficult to falsify data that can be used to distinguish between types of otherwise indistinguishable goods. In this case the "goods" in question may be Web sites, email (spam or legitimate warning?), or privacy policies. Ideally, identity systems can communicate structural information from social networks to create difficult-to-falsify signals. These signals could indicate that a web site has a history of reliable behavior, just as good grades indicate that a potential employee has a history of hard work.

First and foremost, the privacy market does not have adequate signals. At the most fundamental level, "protecting privacy" is a vague promise. For example, the privacy-enhancing technology market boom of the nineties included privacy protection that ranged from Zero Knowledge's provably secure and private email to Microsoft Passport's concentration of information in one location. Even when privacy can be defined and specified, e.g., through machine-readable P3P policies, a signaling problem remains.

The privacy-signaling problem has been described in formal mathematical terms, and illustrates that the market for privacy cannot function without an external forcing function. A model of the market with fluctuating numbers of reliable privacy-respecting merchants illustrates that the market will not necessarily reach equilibrium where it is efficient for consumers to read privacy policies. As the cost of investigating the privacy policy increases, merchant respect of their own policies varies, and thus the reliability of what is read changes, there is no stable equilibrium under which consumers should read privacy policies.

Data compiled from privacy behaviors suggest that whatever the risks and why ever the reason, the risks of privacy are in fact discounted in consumer decision-making. In fact, individuals not only immediately discount privacy risk, but they increase their discount rate over time. That is, if there is an immediate small benefit and a great cost in the future, people choose the immediate benefit. This is particularly interesting considering the rapid rate of increase in identity theft that suggests the risks increase over time.

Privacy can be good or bad for individuals, if the information obtained by others is used to lower prices or to extend privileges. In particular, the opposite of privacy in the market is not necessarily information; the opposite of privacy is price discrimination. In markets where there are zero marginal cost (e.g., information markets) firms must be able to extract consumer surplus by price discrimination. This means that the firms cannot charge what they pay, at the margin, but must charge what the consumer is willing to pay. What are privacy violations to the consumer may be necessary pricing data to the merchant. Accurate signaling information, while useful for the market may not be in the interest of firms and thus never receive support.

Imagine that a company produces some numbers of useful things, say software packages. After the code is written, the only cost is to write the software on a CD, or even host it on a web page. There are many people who will buy the software, and the trick to making the most money is to sell the software for the right amount. Knowing just how much a person or institution will pay for something means knowing about that person. So the opposite of privacy, for a company, is not surveillance. The opposite of privacy is extremely accurate pricing.

There are two things that enabled by exact price information: price discrimination and bundling.

Price discrimination is common to anyone who has purchased an airline ticket, or a sporting event ticket. Careful planners on tight budgets buy airline tickets early, and stay over Saturday. The company traveler or well-paid buying on a whim can pay a high price. In this way, the airplane is filled with the greatest possible revenue. Once the airline company has purchased the plane; built the infrastructure; and paid the people the cost of an additional seat is almost zero. So the airline can afford to fill a few seats with low-paying passengers. These low-paying passengers can sometimes pay less than the average fixed cost and still be profitable.

Yet someone has to pay above average fixed cost, or the system will not work. By having complex fare schedule, airlines can fill plans with the most people and the most profit. Simply charging everyone the higher fare would leave many of us at home, the seats empty; and the airline in a worse condition. Charging everyone the lower price would fill the seats, but not cover the cost of flying the plane. The reason selling those seats at a low price makes sense is that marginal cost of having one more person on the plane is extremely low.

Price discrimination is the ability to charge a person exactly what an item is worth to that person. One way to get price discrimination is to auction off everything. Each person could buy airline tickets, with the price fluctuating as individuals entered and exited the auction. Yet this requires coordination: everyone would have to buy at the same time. So instead, merchants have used timing, advertisement, packaging, and other mechanisms to attempt price discrimination.

Airlines are not the only industry to use timing for price discrimination. *Harry Potter and the Order of the Phoenix* could be purchased full price by those staying up until midnight at the bookstore. Another way to obtain a cheaper copy was to wait until the book was resold as used. Those with more patience than cash could sign up to obtain a copy of the library. From full price to free, these options are available for an identical commodity item. Yet the line to pay full price will be hours long for the final book in the summer of 2007.

Merchants can also sell distinct versions of an item. Those who waited months for the paperback paid less, at risk for learning of the death of great wizards on a blog before getting the book themselves.

Alternatively, all the *Potter* books can be packaged, for a larger total price of a lower price per book. Bundling allows producers to sell more goods to more people, by adding lower value goods in with higher value goods. Imagine that there are two books, call them *Philosopher* and *Sorcerer*, and each costs $10 to produce. One customer values *Philosopher* at $10, and *Sorcerer* at $30. The other customer values *Sorcerer* at $10 and *Philosopher* at $30. If each book is sold for $20, then the bookstore sells two books for $40. If they are sold in a package at $40, the store sells four books for $80. In this case, both the customers and the bookstore are better off with bundling.

Bundling becomes potentially more profitable for goods that have a high initial fixed cost for the very first item and low marginal cost for the additional items. For example, after a software package is written, it costs almost nothing to make copies. So obtaining an increase in marginal profit by selling more bundled goods is better for the producer, and often the consumer. Like the airline which is willing to accept less than the average fixed cost for a seat (because the flight is going regardless) the software producer would like to obtain more total income.

For the merchant, it would be ideal to be able to simply know the customer's type. Is this customer rich, with a tendency to take trips on a whim? Does this customer stand in line for each release of the Potter series and would pay double for a first night copy? One way to determine this is to be able to identify every customer, and have a copy of the customer's detailed personal data. A customer who has purchased six books on Anguilla; has a twenty-year wedding anniversary in March; and has a salary of six figures can be charged more for his vacation for two even if he stays over a Saturday night. Allowing that customer to book early, from the perspective of the airlines, is leaving money in the customer's wallet that could go to the airline profits.

The opposite of privacy is not exposure or risk; the opposite of privacy is price discrimination.

The drive to maximize profits is the drive to implement detailed data surveillance. It is true that this may have painful unintended personal or political results. But the tremendous, ubiquitous to the point of almost gravitational force to record, resell, process, and correlate data is simply the force to charge exactly as much as each customer is willing to pay for the same item.

Companies have very limited economic incentive or liability so security is inadequate. Companies have immense economic incentives so privacy is embattled. Yet these same economic actors have a long term need for secure, reliable credentials that will not be created with current economic forces. Coordination, organization, and investment is a secure and reliable identity infrastructure is in all our interests in the long term.

8. Trusting Code and Trusting Hardware

by Bennet Yee

Should we trust hardware any more than we trust code or software? Why? What are the differences?

In order to trust a device or system to perform actions on our behalf, whether it is some form of local data processing (e.g., word processing) or electronic commerce activity (e.g., ordering goods via the Internet), we have to have trust in the devices that perform these actions on our behalf. Certainly, we are confident that our Selectric typewriters will remain uninfected by viruses. By contrast, we cannot have the same level of trust in our word processors regarding viruses. On the other hand, a Selectric has far fewer features than a word processor.

Observing that all software has to run on some hardware and that hardware is often useless without software to run on it, we might think that the distinction between software and hardware is easy to make. With the possible exception of quantum computing, there is no difference between what, in principle, can be computed by systems that perform more (or less) of their work in hardware versus software. The *speed* at which the results are arrived at will, of course, vary, but what is computable is identical.

There are, however, important qualitative distinctions between software and hardware---and "firmware"---that should be taken into account. Hardware tends to have a more limited set of behaviors. This is because what hardware can and cannot do is basically fixed by the design. Software, on the other hand, is changeable and thus has a potentially infinite range of behavior; a software-driven device's behavior cannot be determined once and for all: not only does its behavior depend on what software was originally installed on the device, it also depends on how that software has been modified afterward. That software may be dynamically updated, perhaps by authorized software updates and patches, or perhaps maliciously through computer viruses.

Embedded software (firmware, such as you might find in an automobile) lies somewhere in the middle. Devices controlled by embedded software can sometimes be updated, if the embedded software is stored on chips that allow such updates, e.g., using flash memory or EEPROM chips as opposed to ROM chips, then that embedded software is also vulnerable to being maliciously updated. Yet despite the complexity, there are malicious programs which target firmware. For example, the pharming attack on the wireless router described above is an attack on the embedded software.

The flexibility of software or the ease with which software can be updated is both is its blessing and curse. The positive side is that when a security problem is identified, it is also relatively easy to install more software to fix the problem.

The ease with which software can be changed also makes security more difficult. First, the malleability of software creates an economic incentive for producers to release software before it is fully debugged. Purveyors to ship flawed products, knowing these can be easily fixed in the field. Software malleability also makes it difficult to evaluate any given computer. In order to decide whether to trust a particular device requires a security review or evaluation to determine the vulnerabilities that the device may have, and the current state of the code. Changing the device invalidates the security review or evaluation performed earlier, since new vulnerabilities may have been introduced.

Hardware devices, by their immutable nature, rarely require a re-evaluation. Of course, the ability to trust hardware is also a function of progress in process control. For example, the vaunted steel hull of the Titanic was made with flawed steel. Modern detailed examinations of the wreckage suggest that impurities and weaknesses of the steel made the Titanic far more fragile than any of its designers could have predicted. The steel bucked and cracked because the process controls were inadequate and materials science as much alchemy as established academic domain.   Today even the most complex micro-electronic can and are examined at every stage of production. Thus hardware is re-evaluated on if the operating environment changes beyond what the original evaluation covered, or when the requirements change.

Complex devices can---and do--- surprise us even when they cannot be maliciously changed. It is also far easier to build complex applications using software than using hardware, and complex applications will be harder to specify, harder to implement, harder to debug, and harder to analyze for security vulnerabilities. Complex systems embed flaws, just as the massive production of steel for the Titanic embedded impurities. Software enables the construction of very complex systems.

In engineering, the "KISS principle" adjures designers to Keep It Simple, that is, to look for simple and elegant solutions and avoid complex and baroque ones. Despite the wisdom in this engineering acronym, software designers have developed an industry-wide tendency to add complex features. This complexity often leads to decreased reliability and consequently decreased trustworthiness.

Identity systems suffer from this same systematic problem. *An identity system designed to resolve a specific problem explodes until it is more dangerous than useful.* For example, public key systems were designed to share a specific credential became the Public Key Infrastructure which was to identify all humans in all context.

While software-oriented designs are not inherently less trustworthy than hardware-oriented designs *if they solve the same problem*, software is used to solve larger and more complex problems. Expansion of the code is easier, both initially and after introduction. The inherent complexity of the corresponding solutions makes such systems less trustworthy.

The design, implementation, and deployment of trusted systems can ideally include some hardware components in the Trusted Computing Base (TCB). Currently, most computers included trusted hardware that, properly protected, can be completely trustworthiness throughout the hardware's life cycle. The core reason that the TCB can be trustworthy is that it has tamper-proof hardware. Because of the cryptographic strength of this hardware, home users can be more lax. While companies can continue to invest in more carefully controlled-access facilities, limited network access, and proper procedural security; home users with a TCB can ensure that the hardware's integrity is not violated.

Recall that the hardware and software cannot be perfectly separated. Implementing protections for the software components of the TCB is complex. Not only does the underlying hardware have to be properly protected, but also access to that hardware must be carefully controlled. Properly detecting and controlling physical access to hardware is a far easier task than detecting and controlling accesses to software. No homeowner is without some perimeter defense, even if she never thinks of it in those terms. The relative simplicity of the defense mechanism for hardware makes the maintenance of trustworthiness easier.

However, the Trusted Computer Base is also called the Treacherous Computing Base. Storing identity information in a TCB allows correct identification over the network. However, stored identity information may also require correct identification. Anonymous access to information can be prohibited. In fact, the first documented goal of TCB was not protecting the identity of the computing homeowner, but rather ensuring that any machine on the network was linked with an identifiable entity. A TCB may strip the homeowner of any anonymity, to ensure that the price is always right. Or a TCB may secure cryptographic secrets to limit identity leakage and protect the individual. The technology can be used either way.

9.   Technologies of Identity

Identity management at the most common is the connection between a personal name, address or location, and account.

The most common identity management mechanisms today focus on the certification of a person known in an organization to interact with enterprise systems. With enterprise identity systems, this has expanded into an integrated system of business processes, policies and technologies that enable organizations to facilitate and control their customers' access to critical online applications and resources while protecting confidential personal and business information from unauthorized users. Many companies and some governments already have this level of identity management. Companies are interested in charging for individual services, interacting across organizational lines, targeting advertisement, and leveraging corporate partnerships.

At the second level identity management is the ability to authenticate a set of permanent, long-lived or temporal attributes unique to each individual. The confirmation and use of attributes enables the identified to take actions and interact with others in a safe secure manner. For the purpose of the converged network (text, voice, video, mobile, and fixed) the critical functionality of identity management at this level is to securely deliver customers their content anywhere, anytime, and on any device. For the purpose of digital government, identity management is to securely deliver services to its citizens anywhere, anytime and on any device. The technical requirements are not unalike.

Identity management is at the most profound the systematic identification of a person, role, or payment on the network. Effective identity management at this level implies leveraging confirmation of identity to serve the end points of the network. For the purpose of the government, this means leveraging the unique features of government in the identity realm to manage the nation.

Identity management has three possible dimensions: reach, strength, and level of centralization.

Identity management can be *dedicated*, the level at which institutions without enterprise identity management are currently operating. Identity management is internal, and may depend on a single point of identification for each application. Identity management is used for specific elements of the organization where each point of information is targeted to a particular task. Identity management can be *ubiquitous*, where there is a core set of attributes for each account or identified entity within an account.

Identity management can have different technical strengths. Identity management depends on authentication. The underlying authentication determines the strength of an identity management system: weak or strong.

Authentication is based on three factors. First, it can be something you know. A person may know anything from a weak four digit PIN, to a complex password, or even a cryptographic secret stored in a human readable form.

Second, authentication can be based on something you are. In security literature this corresponds to biometric identification such as a fingerprint or an iris. It may also correspond to something more temporary; for example, landline telephone and pay television authentication is based on location. Are you at the location determined to be subscribing is a question of something you are, i.e., where.

Third authentication can be based on something you physically possess; for example a car key or a smart card.

These elements can be combined. For example, a person holding a remote for a cable TV box in a living, and entering a PIN to authorize a purchase has all three. The remote is what the customer *possesses*, the location is where the customer *is*, and the PIN is what the customer *knows*. Each of these elements can be strengthened independently. However, that which the customer has (the remote) is available to anyone who is present at the location, so the combination is weaker than if the two were independent. For example, a visiting minor may pick up a remote and purchase a video on demand. Adding a PIN requirement prevents this type of purchase. removing the remote requirement, and replacing it with a biometric and PIN would enable portable authentication. For example, travelers might then be able to purchase content in their hotel rooms or for their iPods. Efficacy of identity management depends upon the reliability of the authorization of the critical attribute: age, willingness to pay, location, etc.

A strongly authenticated attribute or identity can be more effectively leveraged at a lower risk than weakly identified identities. Even a strongly authenticated identity can have weakly or strongly authenticated attributes. For example, an address may be strongly authenticated by physically visiting a location, such as by placement of customer premises equipment. However, the ability of the person holding the equipment to authorize release of information may not be as well authenticated. An example of this is telephony. Wireline telephones are placed into a home, and the line in the home can be identified. Yet a friend can make an expensive call while visiting, or a child can accept a collect call from a relative.[13] Thus while the billing address is strongly authenticated the right to authorize payment is weakly authenticated.

---

[13] For example, the high cost of phoning from prison is a serious problem in the US. Families may lose their breadwinner, and then the phone shortly thereafter based on the high cost for collect calls from parties that hold the contracts to provide phone services from prisons. The result is economic and communications isolation.

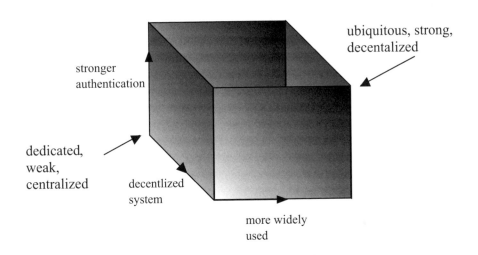

Figure 5: Identity Management Dimensions

Identity management may be strong or weak, centralized or decentralized, ubiquitous or dedicated to a specific purpose. These dimensions are independent and orthogonal. The long-term optimal identity management system is strong, decentralized, and narrowly targeted in order to avoid relying on other systems. The economic incentives are for weak, centralized or federated and thus highly interdependent systems.

The third dimension of identity management is its concentration. Identity management systems can be highly distributed or highly centralized.

A highly centralized view of the world concentrates on a single database. This point of leverage is used to distribute owned or contractually controlled services to a previously identified and associated population.

A decentralized approach leverages customer identification with a set of identified partners to use the customer data to better offer a series of services. This is a service-based rather than a box-centric approach. The ability to bill for services offered by others and delivered by the network is the promise of this approach.

The most decentralized, also called an open approach, leverages information to produce a set of open services that can be utilized (and paid for) by any individual using the open service. For example, a database of authenticating information cane be used to evaluate claims of attribute association by any member of an alliance would be an open identity architecture.

10. Anonymous Identifiers

I know where you live.

This statement implies a threat that any failure in interaction can be met with an expansion beyond the scope of the transactions. That is a mouthful for your average bully. But the simple threat above is based on spheres of activity.

"Anonymous" is the opposite of "uniquely identified." A face in the crowd is anonymous depending on the size of the crowd and the feasibility of the technology to examine the crowd given its size. Today, a face in the crowd will be identifiable to the extent that there is video technology, and the individual facial geometry is recorded and unique.

Anonymity is the opposite of identity. Yet anonymity does not mean that there is no accountability. This is most richly explained in the scenarios. in chapters 14 through 17. Anonymity means that credential authentication does not depend on the intermittent step of identity authentication.

Cookies can be anonymous or function as identifiers. Cookies can be totally anonymous, linking only one request for information to the next.

The inherent value of the cookie itself is its functional: cookies save state.   The cookie distinguishes each browser from the other. Without cookies, it would be impossible to fill a virtual shopping cart and then pay for the goods, as the thread of browsing connections over time would be lost.

When your cookie is linked to purchases and records from one site to another site, then that cookie subverts your anonymity by making connections across domains.

A cookie linked to your New York Times subscription registers on-line reading habits, as does one from Washington Post. That cookie may be linked to personal data entered during registration. That would make the cookie closely associated with personally identifiable information. However, entering one of the well-known and widely shared identifiers based on a favorite blog, a local soccer club or just a common well-known login also yields an identifier. In this case the identified is an *anonym*, instead of an I.D. It links your reading habits to others with the same ID, but you each have a unique cookie. Using these group identifiers is an expression of a desire for privacy.

A cookie that is linked to widely used ID identifies you as part of a statistical group. A blog, it identifies the number of readers who come from the blog and stay. In the soccer club, it identifies everyone associated with that soccer club. If this is a neighborhood club then the people in that club are likely to have similar incomes, and increasingly similar political alignment. The cookie on your machine identifies you as part of a group and an individual in that group. But it does not provide an identifier that can link you to other transactions, domains, or credentials. You are provided a low quality anonymous identifier.

The value of identifying a person as a group member is that it enables targeted ads. By associating yourself with a group, you provide statistical information. The statistical information from the group enables more perfectly targeted advertisement and price discrimination.

Identity stands in for difficulty of physical credential reproduction in the digital realm. Digital anonymous credentials prove that this need not be the case. Identity also provides several secondary effects – a lack of privacy, more efficient marketing, a risk of identity theft, and the ability to reclaim your charge cards in a remote city using only the knowledge in your head.

Cryptography is the art of hiding information using mathematics. Therefore, while the slave's hair may have effectively hidden information, the use of mane instead of math places that particular technique outside the range of encryption. Cryptography can solve the problems of privacy and security simultaneously, while ensuring accountability.

Modern cryptography, using machines and codes too complex to break by even the most brilliant sleight of mind, was born in the turmoil before World War II. First the Italians stole the American substitution code, providing it to the Germans. This provided critical information even before the US entered the war, enabling the brilliance of at least one German general. Before Pearl Harbor, Colonel Bonner Frank Fellers, West Point Graduate and former personal assistant to MacArthur, provided detailed timely information to Washington about British plans. He was diligent from his post in Cairo to investigate every plan of the British Empire. By doing so he provided the information to Field Marshall Rommel as well. No doubt Rommel would have agreed with the post-war citation given to Fellers that noted, "His reports given to the War Department were models of clarity and accuracy." The historical record argues that the accurate information encrypted in weak American ciphers enabled at least one massacre of British forces. The War Department valued Fellers' clarity so much that they cleared his security practices in a review in June 1942 despite British complaints. Fellers was recalled in July of 1942, after the British provided decryptions of his reports to the surprised Americans. Thus on October 23 the 8th Army attack on the German positions led by the Dessert Fox came as a complete surprise. The fox had lost his seventh sense.

Later the tables turned with the well-known breaking of the German Enigma machine and the Japanese Purple code. Alan Turing is rightly famed for designing the first computer, which vastly sped the cracking of specific keys for the German Enigma machine. William and Elizabeth Friedman were the less known husband and wife team who decoded the Enigma-based machines used by the Japanese for their communications before and during World War II.

The ability to read Axis codes allowed the Allies to target and shoot down the plane of Admiral Isoroku Yamamoto 18 April 1943. Yamamoto was educated at Harvard and served as Naval Attaché to the United States in 1925-28. He commanded the Japanese Combined Fleet, and planned the Attack Pearl Harbor as well as being in command at the Battle of Midway. The Battle of Midway was to be a surprise attack, following a feint at Alaska. Because of the breaking of the Japanese code, the feint was doomed to failure and the US Navy attacked and broke the Japanese naval superiority at Midway. That taking advantage of the opportunity required the perseverance, bravery, sacrifice and skill of the forces at Midway should not be understated. The cryptographers made it possible for there to be the possibility of an advantage.

Yamamoto's intelligence and his understanding of American warfare were of such value to the United States that the US risked identifying that the Purple codes were broken through this ambush. How could the Japanese possibly believe sheer luck brought the Americans to Yamamoto's lightly escorted flight? A change in codes could have been disastrous. However, the Japanese were so confident that the Purple codes could never be broken that the codes were never updated.

Similar certainty is embedded in many schemes today, where the risks are lower but the technology more complex. Individuals are assured of perfection in digital signatures and identity schemes. Obviously less is on the line today than global domination in terms of numbers of lives. But the destruction of individual lives in terms of false life-shattering arrests for child pornography based on a stolen credit card, or false convictions of theft based on the perfection of ATM machines is nonetheless terrible for the individuals involved. Yet the blindness to past major risks suggests that systems designers cannot be relied upon to carefully plan for the risk of failure. Systems are oft designed to fail completely or succeed completely, with the risk sometimes going to the party least capable of defending himself – the Unlucky User.

In the physical world there are local failures that feel catastrophic - losing a wallet being the classic. A lost wallet requires contacting any entity that is represented in your wallet. Most importantly, for financial reasons, most people first contact the bank and the credit card company. Yet many of the materials in a wallet or purse are anonymous, such as cash. The loss of cash will not expose a bank account the theft, but neither is it recoverable.

Physical keys are anonymous. Some have stamped numerical identifiers on them. The occasional hotel key still allows the holder to identify the room. Most of us carry keys that cannot be associated with the locks they open.

Anonymous credentials take a different tack on the problem of authentication. By making credentials anonymous the possible influence of subversion is lost. For the imperial Japanese losing Purple was a critical element of losing World War II because the codes encrypted all confidential traffic. For the Unlucky User losing a Social Security Number is the core of losing an identity, because that number is the key to all the financial controls associated with a person. Because of the link to the person and financial records, originally social security numbers were prohibited as identification numbers. For verification, this limitation was printed on every card.

Figure 6: Social Security Card

Note the bottom line: NOT FOR IDENTIFICATION.

It is not the number itself that makes identification the problem. Not the top line, it is the second line: the name associated with the number. The top line provides a number, and that number links taxes paid to benefits due. The second line links all of these to the person associated with the number.

Anonymous credentials in the physical world are very common. Basically any bit of valuable paper without identifying information is an anonymous credential. A dollar is an anonymous credential that proves the right to spend that amount. It is truly a meaningless bit of paper with green ink and some embedded counterfeit protection. Yet it is valuable because the producer, the person holding it, and the merchant, agree upon its value. US currency is accepted many places where the US government has no power: in developing countries, in enemy countries, even in the Soviet Union before its collapse. Other examples of anonymous credentials include tickets to Broadway performances, movie tickets, most bus passes, coupons and those authenticating tags that are not supposed to be removed until the mattress makes it home.

Anonymous credentials are difficult in the digital world because copying is costless, easy and ubiquitous in the digital world. To open a file is to make temporary copies in the cache, after calling the longer-lived copy from the hard drive. Physical anonymous credentials depend on being difficult to copy to maintain their value. If it were trivial to Xerox dollars, inflation would be have to be measured daily.

Some credentials that could clearly be anonymous are linked to identity. Grocery store coupons could be anonymous. Most coupons are anonymous – 50 cents discount for the purchase of chocolate chips if you buy butter. Yet coupons printed for the customer when the customer uses a grocery store discount card are not always anonymous. The value for the customer is printed on the coupon, in large obvious print. The value for the merchant is knowing their customer. Their customer may provide statistical information for other customers: what else did that customer buy? What promotions should be linked? Knowledge can guide advertisements: are their customers more likely to own cats or dogs? The knowledge of the customer can be linked to other databases: what movies appeal people who fit the profiles of their customers, and thus where should they place ads?

Airline tickets were once effectively anonymous. Airline travel now requires the provision of a government-issued i.d. Of course, the criminals have most reliable identification. The major result of requiring identity in airline travel has been to prevent the resale of tickets. Before 2001, tickets could be easily transferred if one person could not use a ticket and wanted to resell it. There was a small industry of people buying cheap "travel in advance" tickets and selling them. Online auctions changed the potential of that industry from small retail services to wholesale arbitrage. If you have a ticket, then the online auctions can match you with a buyer.

Linking identity to airline travel does not increase safety. If the more trusted passengers were indeed given less scrutiny any attacker would begin planning by obtaining a more trusted identity. By creating a list of "more trusted" passengers based on untrustworthy documents the security of air travel is decreased. All of the 9-11 hijackers flew under assumed identities, identities of valuable Saudi customers. The failure on 9-11 was a systematic failure to take precaution, and the ability of attackers to take advantage of business as usual. The check-in agents flagged the hijackers in Maine, and made them check in again in Massachusetts. Yet there was no heightened alert. There was no basis for the agents to refuse boarding. Changing business as usual to create a group of trusted passengers presents another vulnerability in business as usual.

Why then does airline travel require identification? Adding identifiers to airline tickets makes them non-transferable. It does not prevent crime. It prevents commerce.

As long as an airline ticket was an anonymous credential (that is, there was a name but the passenger did not have to prove association with that name) there was a secondary market in airline tickets. Brokers could buy tickets two or three weeks in advance and then resell them. If the broker bet correctly and was able to resell all the tickets purchased, then the broker made money. If the broker could only sell a few, the broker lost money. The advent of widespread consumer-to-consumer commerce, first on Usenet and now on dedicated web sites, made the chances of that broker selling all the tickets very high. Effectively brokers' opportunities for arbitrage were vastly increased by the reduced search and transactions cost of the Internet. Adding identity confirmation for airline travel reduced the opportunity for arbitrage, made the market less fluid, and did nothing for security in airline travel.

Similarly proposals to demand identification for bus passes prevent people from sharing bus passes. Currently two or three people could purchase a bus pass and trade it off. With an identification requirement, this becomes impossible.

There is nothing wrong with the airlines or the buses setting prices and insisting that customers stick to the contract. A deal is a deal, after all. Airlines could pursue resellers of named tickets. Bus companies could give drivers the authority to demand identification with the use of a bus pass.

Yet the treatment of identity in these economic situations as if identity were being used to increase security, instead of profit margins, is a very serious problem. When government is watching people travel, and purchase, and trade that is a significant threat to privacy. It is one thing for the bookstore to ask that I not resell a book at risk of being charged a resell premium. It is another for the government to obtain a database of my reading, travel, and leisure time.

The pretense of security places the customer at a bargaining disadvantage. Wanting a grocery store card that is anonymous because Unlucky User doesn't want to risk identity theft is a reasonable option. Wanting a grocery store card that is anonymous when such anonymity is a risk to national security is clearly less reasonable. After all, with an anonymous card the terrorist could buy a large number of over the counter chemicals to produce a toxic chlorine gas crowd. Of course, the fact that such a purchase would not be flagged and indeed, these purchases in American history, have been intended to clean filth from bathrooms makes such theoretical arguments obviously flawed.

Identity is used to day to increase profit by placing risk on consumers of identity theft, fraud, and even wrongful criminal prosecution. Systematic exposure of citizenry to these risks does not enhance national or personal security. However, through price discrimination and targeted advertising there is a market reason for these actions.

Identity misuse is the pollution of the information age. Everyone breathes and lives in a little more risk so that a very few people can obtain marginally increased profit margins. Using identity in a way that exposes Unlucky to harm is as wrong as dumping chemicals in his drinking water.

Anonymous digital credentials illustrate that living without privacy is no more necessary in the information age than living without clean air was necessary in the industrial age.

As with tickets to the theatre and passes to the rides at the fair, there are anonymous generic tickets available on the Internet. No person has to show identification to get into the movie (assuming they are old enough to watch what they have chosen). When we purchase a roll of tickets at the fair, there is no protocol for transferring the right to ride to the children.

The equivalent of paper passes exist on the Internet: unlinked to identity tokens. These are either called digital tokens or proof of work, depending upon how they are made. A distinct reliable party mints tokens. Proof of work tickets are generated by the person who wants to present them.

Anonymous tokens are digitally linked to some value, like one dollar. (The linkage uses public key cryptography is as described in the next section.) Anonymous tokens are strings of bits rather than rectangles of paper. A token is digitally signed, just as currency is traditionally "signed" by the Treasurer of the United States and by the Secretary of the Treasury. Each US dollar also has a series number, and those numbers are unique and sequential. The issuer, usually a bank, signs an anonymous digital token. The bank then keeps a copy of the digital token. When it is spent it goes to the merchant and then back to the bank. Because of the way the token was signed, the bank will recognize it as being signed but cannot connect it to a merchant. The essential observation is that a third party, usually a centralized trusted party, verifies anonymous tokens. Digital tokens can be very strongly authenticated. However, even with the centralized elements, digital tokens can be decentralized. Merchants choose to take tokens or not. Consumers hold their own tokens before they are spent. And of course this is very private.

Tickets are different than tokens. Tickets are generated by evidence of effort. While anonymous tokens are money, tickets are more analogous to manners. As payment is a universal phenomenon, so is appropriate address upon introduction. Liberty Alliance offers the option of being the universal introducer. Tickets allow us to do the digital equivalent of dressing well and being on time. Using computational power, memory accesses, or human interaction to show that a request for services is made in good faith generates tickets.

Tokens, like dollar bills, are relatively expensive to create. A token is associated with the party that signs it. While the spender of a dollar or user of a coupon or distributor of a digital token is not identified, the producer of the dollar, coupon or token is well known.

While a token might be used for an arbitrary payment, tickets can be used to defeat misuse of identifiers by adding a cost to digital introductions. For example, consider spam. Spam is on its own a significant problem in that it consumes vast network and human resources. If the Internet is an attention span economy, then spam is wholesale theft. CipherTrust estimates in 2005 the volume of global email as exceeding 50 billion messages per day. Spam is so profitable that estimates of spam as a percentage of all email has increased even as the total volume of email increases. Estimates of the percent of email sent (not delivered) range from 56% in 2003 to 80% in 2006. Spam is a malicious network activity enabled by the otherwise virtuous cycle of network expansion. As the network expands, spam becomes more profitable, and thus increases. Spam is also a vector for other activities: distribution of malicious code, phishing attacks, and old-fashioned fraud.

The core challenge in defeating spam is that the sender bears almost no cost to send email. The cost is borne by the network service providers and the recipients. In order to solve this problem, proof of work was designed to alter the economics of spam by requiring that the sender commit to a per-email cost.

The core enabling factor of spam is that spam is cheap to send. The negligible cost of sending spam makes solicitations with response rates in the tenths of a percent profitable. Proof of work was deigned to remove the profit from spam.

Proof of work comprises a set of proposals. Different proposals require email senders to require fungible payment, perform a resource-intensive computation, (Dwork and Noar, 1992), perform a series of memory operations (Dwork, Goldberg, and Naor, 2003), or post a bond, (Krihsamurthy and Blackmond, 2004) for each message sent. This section describes the initial proof of work proposal, and details different analysis.

In 1992, the first computational technique for combating junk mail was presented by Cynthia Dwork and Moni Naor. Their fundamental contribution was to link the economics of email with the security and privacy threat of spam. They did this by proposing that to send an email require the computation of some moderately hard, but not intractable, function of the message and some additional information in order to initiate a transmission. Sending an email means initiating a network transmission. Initiating a transmission means gaining access to the resources: the network for transmission, the recipient's storage in an inbox, and the recipient's attention span if the transmission is accepted.

The essence of POW is that "if you want to send me a message, then you must prove your email is worth receiving by spending some resource of your own". Currently, email is a market that has been almost completely broken. Therefore the key property of the POW functions is that they are very expensive for the email sender to solve, but comparatively cheap for the email recipient to verify the solution.

Of course, the time investment in any processing-intensive POW system depends upon the specific platform. Work that might take 20 seconds on a Pentium IV could take several minutes or more on a Pentium II, and be completely infeasible on a mobile phone. To address this problem, a POW pricing function based on accessing large amounts of random access memory as opposed to raw processing power was originally proposed by Cynthia Dwork, Andrew Goldberg, and Moni Naor, with later work creating additional memory-bound mechanisms. Since memory speeds vary much less across machines than CPU speeds, memory-bound functions should be more equitable than CPU-bound functions. While processing speeds can vary by orders of magnitude, Dwork claims a factor of four between fastest and slowest memory operations. The current Microsoft implementation, Penny Black, is designed to be agnostic about the form of work and requires only some form of work.

POW offers one way to prevent spam that allows each of us to select with whom we will openly share our inboxes. Imagine each of us had our own histories and lists of people we have communicated with in the past.

Each person who wanted to connect would have to do some work as an introduction. If we didn't like the email, labeling it as spam or even rather rude, no more email from that address would reach us. This would entirely alter the economics of spam. And it would alter those economics using our own social networks. For example, some people love getting Chicken Soup for the Soul. Others embrace the latest update on wiretapping legislation and practice. No one wants to be fraudulently separated from his or her money.

The alternative anti-spam network technologies are all based on hierarchies. There is no hierarchy that determines who we invite to dinner, and into our cars. Each of us has a right to be absolutely arbitrary and wrong about sharing our individual resources. This autonomy should continue on the network.

Right now, anyone can use a network identifier with very little investment. Your email, your web address, and the commonly shared bandwidth over the Internet are all resources that can be abused by identity stealing network criminals. Either each all contribute a bit to proof of work; or we can built a universal identifier to enable exact numerical assertions of trust for every person on the Internet. Of course, this new identifier is likely to end up being as much as new vector of attack, while anonymous tickets evaluated by each user will be much more difficult to profitably subvert.

11. Digital Signatures

Digital signatures, and the digital keys that create these signatures, are an important tool in creating an infrastructure that could prevent identity theft. A digital signature is based on two digital keys: a secret key and a public key. The individual holds the secret key, and only the individual can know that secret key. Each key is a special kind of number that is very large, consisting of hundred of digits.[14] The keys must be created in pairs, so that for every secret key there is one corresponding public key.

The public key can decrypt or unlock anything encrypted with the secret key. The secret key can decrypt anything encrypted with the public key. Encrypting twice with either key only makes it necessary to decrypt twice with the other key.

Imagine a drop box. A drop box that is open to the public, where anyone can use the public key to open it and place material in. By its nature as a drop box, putting something in is simple. Everyone has the capacity to drop; everyone has access with the key to the drop box. The drop box, the key and the information dropped in it, are of course, all bits. In the digital dimension, dropping in the box is encrypting with the public key. Only the person with the matching secret key can unlock the encrypted material.

Imagine that each drop box has a number associated with it. You have a check to deliver to a particular person. How do you know in which place to drop it? The association between individual and key created by the public key infrastructure -- a way for everyone to know which drop box uniquely belongs to which individual. Thus the infrastructure that associates the key pair to the individual is critical for digital signatures to work.

Retrieving the material requires the individual's single-person secret key that is the other half of the unique pair. In digital terms, this means decrypting that material that was dropped in through encrypting with the associated public key.

The ability to retrieve is created by the knowledge of the secret key. The association of the secret key, the public key and the person who knows the secret key is created by the public key infrastructure – the PKI.

PKI can be implemented in practice to mean a single identity for all uses in the digital realm: to send and receive email, to authorize payments, to log in at work, or at a government website. In the original vision, PKI would have been ubiquitous in that there would be a single great identity hierarchy,

---

[14] The secret key can be held on any type of computing device: a smart card, a computer, or a mobile phone. The key can be unlocked by any type of authentication; for example, biometrics on a smart card or a pass phrase on a computer.

like one giant phone book for everyone and every institution on the Internet. Anyone who has tried to look up an old friend using Internet white pages realizes how difficult it is to associate exactly one name with one unique number and have no confusion or overlap.

In the original PKI vision, each person would have one pair of keys (a secret and the corresponding public key) that corresponds to his or her "true name." Obviously that has not and cannot happen; however there are a many smaller implementations of smaller PKIs in companies and commerce. For example, the lock on the browser window is a result of a set of competing PKI creating by companies that sell the authentication of the websites with these locks. [15] The proposals for a single national ID all depend on this fundamental idea.

A PKI has two core things: a cryptographic record of the public key of the key pair, and a way to link that record to a larger database of attributes, credentials or identifiers. Recall that the possession of the secret key authenticates the link between the public and the secret key.

However, computers are not as seamless as human beings. So linking a person to a computer record to a larger database is not so easy if you are linking in human terms.

So developing a system that identifies humans in computer terms is not trivial. We identify each other by context, by integrating information. Humans build on context. Computers determine by categorization and parsing. People integrate, computers parse.

The Public Key Infrastructure

A PKI can prevent identity theft by having secure key storage and specified uses. Or a PKI can make identity theft worse though weak security for key storage and strong liability for digital signatures. PKI can enable weak, centralized identity systems or decentralized strong dedicated identity systems. Taking public keys and stapling them onto off-line identities should not be the goal of a Public Key Infrastructure. Obviously, no one suggested an Infrastructure in this manner. Instead, PKI was described as a "digital signature". "Digital signatures" is a powerful metaphor; in fact, too powerful. The signature metaphor implies that everyone has exactly one for every occasion, like a hand written signature. Cryptographic keys can be thought of as physical keys, for all the possible different locks and doors in life. Cryptographic keys can also be thought of credentials, for movie tickets to lifetime memberships.

---

[15] The browser lock indicates that the transmissions are being encrypted and thus cannot be simply read off the wire. The most common use of this encryption technology (Called Secure Sockets Layer) is to protect credit card numbers as they are transmitted over the Internet.

Public keys are widely used today, for example, to generate the confidentiality as indicated with the lock icon on the browser. Public key infrastructures are a way to connect those numbers (e and d above) to a meaningful person or entity. The problem is that the meaning was not considered before the infrastructure was built.

The original suggestion was for a single digital PKI. The original proposal for PKI was X509. The original linking of public keys, which can provide authentication for authorization, was the link to identity from a public key. Of course, in the physical would few people have exactly one key? The history of certificates in PKI provides, in condensed form, what the future history of identity might be.

X509 was the original PKI proposal. X509 proposed that each person has a "distinguished name" and an associated public key. Each person would have a set of attributes associated with an identity. The key would be linked first to identity then to the associated attributes. The attributes would then determine the rights of the identified person: employee, Girl Scout, professor.

X.509 was the original all-digital secure identity infrastructure proposal. It failed in the marketplace. No one party was trusted by every other party to set up the system. Even were the system constructed, companies did not want employee access to depend upon the same key that is used by the Girl Scouts. There are different risks, requirements for confidentiality, and organizational structures associated with different credentials.

X509 assumed a centralized enrolling party. Consider your own enrollments. Mine include an employer, video rental by mail, various online publications, blogs, domains that I administer, and a grocer. No single party can verify each and every attribute for all possible uses. My employer needs to authenticate me very well for me to alter my benefits. However, the worst case for the movie rental company is that someone absconds with three DVDs. My employer also has no basis for investigating my DVD rentals. Yet, with one identifier, the history of DVD rentals might be as much a part of the employment process as are credit checks today.

Physical credentials allow delegation (unfortunately, at times accidental delegation). A movie rental card that is dropped is as useful as a movie rental card that is handed to the teen-ager in the home. Delegation is common in the online world as well, as every assistant with a supervisor's password knows so well. X509 necessarily limited delegation. Because there was one key per person, delegating your one secret key of the key pair would give anyone all your rights. Any delegation key under X509 was a delegation for your entire identity. So to give a colleague the right to sign internal memos in your name meant giving that colleague all your rights (credit cards, health record access, etc) for all time or until you re-establish your identity. Parental rights would be delegated with movie rental rights, there being only one key pair.

The concentration of all identity information with a single public key would have created significant recovery problems. If all data are digital, and the digital identifier is lost or no longer valid, how is recovery possible? The ideal of the single PKI was fundamentally flawed.

While the single universal PKI in the form of X509 did not succeed, there are many distinct PKI instantiations. Different companies built and control their own authentication mechanisms, and these include both devices and humans. Devices clearly do not have "distinguished names" in the form of machine addresses, serial numbers, and retailer-provided identifiers. The ubiquitous UPC code has been expanded so that not only every computing device but also every pair of socks and disposable razor can have unique identifiers. Since socks and razors do not have autonomy they don't interact in different social spheres, but these unique identifiers can be quite useful in a supply chain.

Recall that, like the common UPC on socks, credentials do not have to be associated with identity. One proposal includes privacy-enhanced credentials. In various instantiations (most famously by Stephen Brands) a public key can be linked to a set of credentials. In this case, the individual only shares information on the relevant credential. There is still one key, but the key is used to authenticate attributes, not identify a person in order to imply attributes.

Brands' system allows individual's choice in what attributes are shared with whom, even if another party stores the attributes. This resolves, in a limited way, the problem of recovery. Losing a purse is a terrible thing. However, you are unlikely to lose your purse, cell phone, wallet and change your address at the same time. If this happens, then recovery should be expensive. Recovery should be difficult and require physical presence because this event is extremely rare. Using these blinded credentials has an advantage. It is possible to use a phone or PDA to sign specific credentials. Sometimes, it is only one credential that matters.

> On vacation, I went to Cozumel one week with my children, then one and five. We stayed in an all-inclusive resort with a wonderful children's' programs, and diving off the pier. Relaxation was the operative word. On the flight back we were sitting up front. All around me were a group of contractors who were consuming alcohol and flirting with the flight attendant. The children were good, but this required active parenting as the adults became louder and somewhat inappropriate. One of the things these other passengers were bragging about was their acumen in avoiding taxes, including writing off the cost of this particular trip as a business expense. After some time one turned to me and asked, in a gregarious if drunken manner, what I did. Having a dry sense of humor, I told him I was an auditor for the IRS. After a bit of silence, he replied, "Really?" I laughed and explained that actually no, I was a professor at Harvard with expertise in Internet

commerce. I was just joking. They insisted on selecting a drink, carried my luggage from the plane to the baggage carousel, and praised my kids on the flight. Finally, I told them what happens in Mexico stays in Mexico and that I could honestly say that I would never, ever audit them. (Given that I did not know their names, even had I wanted to change careers, I would not have been able to audit them.)

The point of this tale is that the other passengers had a set of credentials. The other passengers on the flight with me knew my identifier: Jean. The passengers knew that I had two children, and where I spent my vacation. Having spent something like an hour next to me, they had a pretty good idea of my parenting style. Yet they could not use this rich set of credentials to ascertain another (my job). This kind of isolation of credentials can make identity theft more difficult.

Affiliation is powerful. Credential cryptography[16] is a type of public key cryptography that is particularly useful at proving affiliation.

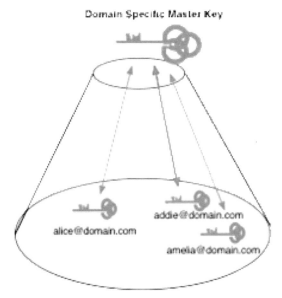

Figure 7: Identity Credentials Cryptographically Confirmed with Email

A cryptographic key in the world of identity is itself only a number or a series of letters. All by themselves, these numbers prove nothing. Credential-based cryptography can prove, for example, that I am an IU professor and not an IRS auditor.

---

[16] Credential cryptography is usually called "identity cryptography", since any random string including a name can be used as the public key. However, the use of the phrase "identity cryptography" would be quite confusing, so I utilize the less widely used phrase credential cryptography.

As with other public keys, there is a need for some connection between the key and the associated attribute. With credential cryptography, that means that there is some third party which authenticates the claimed affiliation or credential. In the case above, that third party would be the university. The university could generate private keys associated with each credential: professor, student, etc. The ability to use the private key generated by the third party would prove the affiliation.

Any third party can use credential cryptography to confirm any particular credential or attribute using a simple string. For example, the ISP can confirm that you come from a stable Internet address. A credit card company can confirm that you have the right to charge without the requirement that you provide your charge account number, or any information that could be reused in a manner that creates risk.

Using credential cryptography instead of filling in forms, all that would be needed to guarantee payment would be a signed email. That email may be signed with a simple cryptographic credentials, e.g. Fandango, can provide a ticket to the movies without having anything from the purchaser but a digitally signed email. The cost of the movie ticket would be authorized using credential cryptography but Fandango need not develop a profile that enables anyone who can obtain access to steal your credit card. Using this system, a person can change emails as often as desired, but then authenticate that email to the credit providing authority. Ideally, if the credit authority errs in accessing a charge, the credit card company could then be liable.

Emails have an advantage over passive provision of reusable information in that they are interactive. Instead of pushing a button on one screen, there can be a requirement for an exchange. You receive and respond to an email in order to enable a credit charge. This is a transaction where there is increased privacy, increased interaction and increased security. The cryptographic credential would require interaction in this case. So identity theft would not be invisible -- it is easy to fake an email address from an account. It is impossible to fake a digitally signed email without the secret key. And it is very close to impossible for anyone to prevent an individual from receiving an email. (A trusted insider working for the recipient's email provider could delete the email after it was received.) So, the individual with the email would get a message with every attempt to charge.

Anyone can create multiple emails so that the failure of one credential would not harm the others. Recall each credential can be linked to an email, or one email linked to many credentials. With purely digital transactions Jean the professor would not be linked to Jean the parent; and indeed no first purchase need be linked with a second.

The reliability of this system depends upon the ability of the credit charging entity to enroll the correct email with the correct account. And enrollment fraud is the essence of identity theft. Enrollment is critical to any successful identity system.

Identity based cryptography can link many emails to one attribute (can charge things to the VISA international clearinghouse) or many attributes to one email. Because the signatures can be compound, any email can prove as many or as few things as the sender wants. For example, the AARP and MasterCard might sign an email. Alternatively, you might carry a phone filled with credentials just as your phone is filled with telephone numbers. Some of these will be anonymous, as with digital cash. Some of these will reflect a debit account, such as a check. Others will indicate your right to draw on a line of credit. Large or unusual purchases may require additional authentication, through interaction over email or proving to your phone that it is indeed you.

The biometrics primer of Chapter 12 describes how biometrics are particularly useful distributed as opposed to centralized. If you have to authenticate yourself to your phone with a fingerprint, using your stolen phone would be more difficult. If that digitized fingerprint record were then stored centrally then anyone could steal the data that digital fingerprint record and forge fingerprints.

End Note: What Are Public Keys

Public key cryptography is based on the circular nature of constrained mathematical spaces. Of course, we use constrained mathematical spaces every day and every minute. The time on the clock never goes past 12:00, or 24:00. The time is never 24:01, and the date is never December 32nd.

Adding 365 days (or 366 during a leap year) to one day in the year results in the same date, one year later. Similarly, it is possible to construct a closed or circular counting system with any number. When that number is prime (imagine having 13 hours) then the counting systems has some most amazing properties. The most interesting, in credential terms, is described in the next paragraph.

First, for ease of reading, represent any closed space like this: mod n. In this case, the clock can be thought of as mod 12 or mod 24, and the number of days is a non-leap calendar year is mod 365. For any number (call it a for any) in a space defined a by prime number (p for prime, so mod p) .

$$a^{(p-1)} = a \ (mod \ p)$$

It is possible to combine two prime numbers, and creating a larger but still constrained space. This is like combining months to create a larger, but still constrained, year. To use some small number examples, 13 is prime, so: $4^{12} = 13*16777215+1$. Similarly $3^6 = 7*104+1$.

Ron Rivest made a magnificent recognition that it is possible to combine two of these[17]. The result was that for any message M there can be

---

[17] This is a vast and gross, but potentially useful, simplification.

two numbers e and d, so that M^{e*d} (mod(p-1)(q-1)) = M(mod(p-1)(q-1)). These two numbers, e and d, are the heart of public key cryptography. In this case, e is the secret key and d is the public key.

Basically, Ron Rivest found a way to wind the clock forward and backwards in a consistent way. Every person has a different set of clocks, two complementary clocks. And winding up one required unwinding the other. One clock is public; one is secret.

Because their complementary nature these clocks or keys solve the problem of key distribution. Two people can communicate without needing to set up a unique key. Public keys do *not* solve the problem of identification. That I can have a public key does not prove any of my attributes except that I do, in fact, have a public key.

Recall that for public key cryptography, keep one number secret and publicize the other. Thus anyone can communicate in a secure manner with anyone else because the initiator of the communication can simply use the public key of the recipient. Just as anyone can send mail to anyone else, the initiator simply has to know the recipient's email. However, as phishing and spam so painfully illustrate, understanding the connection between the key to communication and the person with whom you think you are communicating is not trivial.

12. Strengths and Weaknesses of Biometrics

Elaine M. Newton[18]

Introduction

In general, there are three approaches to authenticating an individual's identity. In order of most secure and convenient to least secure and convenient, they are as follows:

Something you are: a biometric such as a fingerprint.

Something you know: a PIN, such as an ATM bank account password.

Something you have: key, token, card, such as an ID card.

Any combination of these approaches can potentially further heighten security.

Facial recognition software, fingerprint readers, hand geometry readers, and other forms of biometrics appear increasingly in systems with mission-critical security. Given the widespread consensus in the security community that passwords and magnetic-stripe cards accompanied by PINs have weaknesses, biometrics could well be ensconced in future security systems.

This document begins with a definition of biometrics and related terms. It then describes the steps in the biometric authentication process, and reviews issues of template management and storage. The appendix concludes with a brief review of mainstream biometric applications.

---

[18] as adapted from John D. Woodward, Katherine W. Webb, Elaine M. Newton et al., Appendix A, "Biometrics: A Technical Primer," "Army Biometric Applications: Identifying and Addressing Sociocultural Concerns," RAND/MR-1237-A, Santa Monica, CA: RAND 2001. Copyright RAND 2001.

Overview

A biometric is any *measurable, robust, distinctive* physical characteristic or personal trait that can be used to identify, or verify the claimed identity of, an individual. Biometric authentication, in the context of this report, refers to automated methods of identifying, or verifying the identity of, a living person.

The italicized terms above require explanation.

Measurable means that the characteristic or trait can be easily presented to a sensor and converted into a quantifiable, digital format. This allows for the automated matching process to occur in a matter of seconds.

The robustness of a biometric is a measure of the extent to which the characteristic or trait is subject to significant changes over time. These changes can occur as a result of age, injury, illness, occupational use, or chemical exposure. A highly robust biometric does not change significantly over time. A less robust biometric does change over time. For example, the iris, which changes very little over a person's lifetime, is more robust than a voice.

Distinctiveness is a measure of the variations or differences in the biometric pattern among the general population. The higher the degree of distinctiveness is, the more unique the identifier. The highest degree of distinctiveness implies a unique identifier. A low degree of distinctiveness indicates a biometric pattern found frequently in the general population. The iris and the retina have higher degrees of distinctiveness than hand or finger geometry.

The application helps determine the degree of robustness and distinctiveness required. The system's ability to match a sample to a template is sometimes referred to as the biometric's reliability.

Systems can be used either to identify people in a consensual or non-consensual manner - as when faces are scanned in public places - or to verify the claimed identity of a person who presents a biometrics sample in order to gain access or authorization for an activity. The following section expands on this issue.

"Living person" distinguishes biometric authentication from forensics, which does not involve real-time identification of a living individual.

Identification and Verification

Identification and verification differ significantly. With identification, the biometric system asks and attempts to answer the question, "Who is X?" In an identification application, the biometric device reads a sample and compares that sample against every template in the database. This is called a "one-to-many" search (1:N). The device will both make a match and subsequently identify the person or it will not make a match and not be able to identify the person.

Verification is when the biometric system asks and attempts to answer the question, "Is this X?" after the user claims to be X. In a verification application, the biometric device requires input from the user, at which time the user claims his identity via a password, token, or user name (or any combination of the three). This user input points the device to a template in the database. The device also requires a biometric sample from the user. It then compares the sample to or against the user-defined template. This is called a "one-to-one" search (1:1). The device will either find or fail to find a match between the two.

Identification applications require a highly robust and distinctive biometric; otherwise, the error rates falsely matching and falsely non-matching user's samples against templates cause security problems and inhibit convenience. Identification applications are common where the end-user wants to identify criminals (immigration, law enforcement, etc.) or other "wolves in sheep's clothing." Other types of applications may use a verification process.3 In many ways, deciding whether to use identification or verification requires a trade-off: the end-user's needs for security versus convenience.

In sum, biometric authentication is used in two ways: to prove who you are or who you claim you are and to prove who you are not (e.g., to resolve a case of mistaken identity).

Three Basic Elements of All Biometric Systems

All biometric systems consist of three basic elements:
1. Enrolling an individual--the process of collecting biometric samples from an individual, (the "enrollee")-- and subsequently generating her template.
2. Creating templates--the data representing the enrollee's biometric.
3. Matching -- the process of comparing a live biometric sample against one or many templates in the system's database.
Performance refers to the ability of a biometric system to correctly match, or identify individuals.

Enrollment

Enrollment is the crucial first stage for biometric authentication because it generates a template that will be used for all subsequent matching. Typically, the device takes three samples of the same biometric and averages them to produce an enrollment template. Enrollment is complicated by the fact that a users' familiarity with a biometric device usually improves performance because they know how to place themselves in front of or onto a sensor, but enrollment is usually the first time the user is exposed to the device.

Environmental conditions also affect enrollment. Enrollment should take place under conditions similar to those expected during the routine matching process. For example, if voice verification is used in an environment where there is background noise, the enrolling system should capture voice templates in the same environment.

In addition to user and environmental issues, biometrics themselves change over time. Many biometric systems account for these changes by continuously averaging. Templates are averaged and updated each time the user attempts authentication.

Templates

The biometric device stores the data captured when enrolling a person as a template. The device uses a proprietary algorithm to extract features appropriate to that biometric from the enrollee's samples. Templates are only a record of distinguishing features, sometimes called minutiae points, of a person's biometric characteristic or trait. For example, templates are not an image or record of the actual fingerprint or voice.4 In basic terms, templates are numerical representations of key points taken from a person's body. They can be thought of as very long passwords that can identify a body part or behavior.

The template usually occupies a small amount of computer memory (and is smaller than the original image) and thus allows for quick processing, a key feature of making biometric authentication practical.

The template must be stored somewhere so that subsequent templates, created when a user tries to access the system using a sensor, can be compared. Some biometric experts claim it is impossible to reverse-engineer, or recreate, a person's print or image from the biometric template.

Matching

Matching is the comparison of two templates: the one produced at the time of enrollment (or at previous sessions, if there is continuous updating) and the one produced "on the spot" as a user tries to gain access by providing a biometric sample via a sensor.

There are three ways a match can fail:
Failure to enroll / Failure to acquire.
False match.
False nonmatch.
Both failure to enroll (during enrollment) and failure to acquire (prior to matching) are failures to extract distinguishing features appropriate to that

technology. For example, a small percentage of the population fails to enroll in fingerprint-based biometric authentication systems. There are two primary reasons for this failure: the individual's fingerprints are not distinctive enough to be picked up by the system, or the distinguishing characteristics of the individual's fingerprints have been altered because of the individual's age or occupation, e.g., as might happen with an elderly bricklayer.

False match (FM) and false nonmatch (FNM) are frequently referred to by the misnomers "false acceptance" and "false rejection," respectively, but the latter pair of terms are application-dependent in meaning. FM and FNM are application-neutral terms that describe the matching process between a live sample and a biometric template.

A false match occurs when a sample is incorrectly matched to a template in the database (i.e., an imposter is accepted). A false nonmatch occurs when a sample is incorrectly not matched to a truly matching template in the database (i.e., a legitimate match is denied). People deploying biometric systems calculate rates for FM and FNM and use them to make tradeoffs between security and convenience when choosing a system or tuning its parameters. For example, a heavy security emphasis errs on the side of denying legitimate matches and does not tolerate acceptance of imposters. A heavy emphasis on user convenience results in little tolerance for denying legitimate matches but tolerates some acceptance of imposters.

Template Management, Storage and Security

Template management is critically linked to privacy, security, and convenience. All biometric authentication systems face a common issue: biometric templates must be stored somewhere. Templates must be protected to prevent identity fraud and to protect the privacy of users. Privacy is affected when additional information is stored about each user along with the biometric template.

Possible locations template storage include
- the biometric device itself,
- a central computer that is remotely accessed,
- a plastic card or token via a bar code or magnetic stripe,
- RFID (Radio Frequency Identification Device) cards and tags,
- optical memory cards,
- PCMCIA (Personal Computer Memory Card International Association) cards, or
- smart cards.

In general, transmitting biometric data over communications lines reduces system security. Such transmission renders the data vulnerable to the same interception or tampering possible when any data is sent "over the wire." On the other hand, a network or central repository may be needed for some applications where there are multiple access points or when there is a need to confirm information with another node or higher authority. Biometrics are more secure when stored under the control of the authorized user, such as on a smart card, and used in verification applications. Cards have varying degrees of utility and storage memory.

Smart cards are the size of credit cards and have an embedded microchip or microprocessor chip. The chip stores electronic data that can be protected using biometrics. In terms of ease of use, there are two types of smart cards: contact and contactless smart cards. The term "smart card" implies a standard card that must be inserted into a reader. American Express Blue is an example of a smart card that requires reader insertion. A contactless or wireless smart card only has to be placed near an antenna to carry out a transaction.[19] This is particularly useful for passing through an area where the person carrying the card may pass multiple times a day, or where their may have secondary tasks that require the use of the person's hands. Yet the convenience also can create risks, as the signal is broadcast. This risk is physically small albeit in an extremely small range. The risk can also be completely mitigated by encrypting the interaction between the card and the reader. The option of smart-card based encryption for authentication has become eminently feasible with the decrease in the cost of computing power.

The number of uses of the database also affects security for template database storage: will it have a unique use or will it be used for multiple security purposes?

For example, a facilities manager might use a fingerprint reader for physical access control to the building. The manager might also want to use the same fingerprint template database for his employees to access their computer network. Should the manager use separate databases for these different uses, or is he willing to risk accessing employee fingerprints from a remote location for multiple purposes?

Additional security features can be incorporated into biometric systems to detect an unauthorized user. Because unauthorized users malicious entities appearing to be harmless, they are sometimes called "wolves", as in *a wolf in sheep's clothing*. For example, a "liveliness test" tries to determine whether the biometric sample is being read from a live person versus a faux body part or body part of a dead person. Liveliness tests are done in many ways. The device can check for such things as heat, heartbeat, or electrical capacitance.[20]

---

[19] For a detailed discussion of smart cards, see Ratha and Bolle (1999).

[20] Electrical capacitance has proved to be the best and least reproducible method for effectively identifying a live person.

Other security features include encryption of biometric data and the use of sequence numbers in template transmission. A template with such a number out of sequence suggests unauthorized use.

In general, verification applications provide more security than identification applications because a biometric and at least one other piece of input (e.g., PIN, password, token, user name) are required to match a template and the corresponding record. In essence, it is a second layer of security.

Verification provides a user with more control over his data and over the process when the template is stored only on a card. Such a system would not allow for clandestine, or involuntary, capture of biometric data because the individual would know each time, where, and to what system s/he were submitting their biometric. Verification applications with storage (and possibly matching, too) of a biometric template on a card are potentially more palatable to the public (for privacy, convenience, and security concerns) and more secure than identification applications or applications with a repository for many reasons:[21]

There is no large centralized storage location of templates, which could be abused or hacked. An administrator should regard even distributed databases as "honey pots" for hackers and leave open the possibility of abuse.[22] They require the user's consent to capture data.[23] Being in possession of a card adds a layer of security Further, requiring a password can also enhance security.[24]

Because the search seeks only a match against one template in the database, verification applications require less processing time and memory than identification.

---

[21] Security also depends on other factors, such as the care taken to safeguard tokens and passwords and to ensure that transmissions of biometric data are adequately protected.

[22] This primer does not cover standards for interoperability or so-called "plug and play" applications because this subject is tangential to the project. This appendix relies heavily on the following sources: Hawkes and Hefferman (1999) and Wayman (1999c, 19TK). See also Jain, Bolle, and Pankanti (1998).

[23] See, e.g., Appendix B, Program Reports, Fort Sill Biometrically Protected Smart Card.

[24] Image files of fingerprints may be of interest to an organization (such as the FBI or a bank) because of their law enforcement or security applications. In the case of fingerprints, the military may want to keep both electronic image files of the fingerprint as well as the biometric templates. The image files are too large to be used for biometric applications but would be useful for forensic purposes. Moreover, an organization might want to store image files to give it greater technical flexibility. For example, if the FBI did not keep image files of enrollees, it might have to physically reenroll each individual if the FBI decided to change to a different proprietary biometric system. Image files are also known as raw data or the corpus.

Biometric Applications

Most biometric applications fall into one of nine general categories. First there are financial services (e.g., ATMs and kiosks) to limit risks by using biometrics to provide authentication to data. The second large class is to evaluate the right of individuals to make certain movements and cross borders. These are most widely proposed for immigration and border control (e.g., points of entry, pre-cleared frequent travelers, passport and visa issuance, asylum cases).

The use of biometrics where the physical entity is authenticated is broad. In social services biometrics provide fraud prevention in entitlement programs. In health care biometrics offer security measure for privacy of medical records. Biometrics are used for physical access control for a variety of institutions, (e.g., institutional, government, and residential).

Biometrics are also used for narrow replacements for traditional problems of verification. Applications here include time and attendance where biometrics are used as, replacement of time punch card. Biometrics are widely proposed as solutions to problems in computer security including personal computer access, network access, Internet use, e-commerce, and e-mail authentication.

In addition, biometrics have been proposed as an enabling underlying service in telecommunications to limit mobile phone fraud, authenticate callers into call centers, strengthen the security of phone cards, and enable televised shopping.

Finally biometrics have been embraced by law enforcement for us in criminal investigation, national ID, driver's license, correctional institutions/prisons, home confinement, and are integrated into smart gun designs.

Biometrics are any measurable physical feature that can be used to identify or classify a single person or set of people. Some biometrics are considered attributes, for example, age is a biological attribute that is not generally used for authentication. In the physical realm, age is often authenticated by observation, as anyone who has reached the age of being to purchase alcohol without proof of maturity can affirm.

Biometrics have increasingly come to refer to the basic authentication that is possible when an individually is properly enrolled. Biometrics have different relative strengths, but the entropy provided by a biometric in al cases is less than that of a weak password. What is unique about biometrics is that these are fundamentally tied to the body.

The tie to the body does not confirm the accuracy of a corresponding digital record. Enrollment is to no small degree more difficult in biometric systems. Enrollment requires physical presence and a readable biometric. While the most obvious failure to enroll would be loss of limb or eye, there are more chronic difficulties. Particularly the elderly have difficulties in enrollment. The aged frequently do not have readable fingerprints. They are more likely to have cataracts or other medical problems that prohibit the use of retinal scans. While biometrics are the most effective at preventing duplicate enrollment; biometrics also have the most problematic enrollment.

Protection is not possible with biometric data. In any place the body is, the biometric can be read. Fingerprints are left on glasses, and can be reproduced with a heating element and a gummy bear. Retina scans are more intrusive, and are unlikely to be made surreptitiously. Corporations may choose to use the same biometrics for different risks. For example, fingerprints and hand geometry are collected at Walt Disney World. The same data should not then be used to protect a person's life savings. Raw biometrics cannot be recovered. Biometrics are "the password you can never change."

Unlike the case with asymmetric authentication, raw biometrics with centralized storage require that authenticating data be provided for authentication to occur. Therefore, each time authentication occurs with the biometric, the recipient obtains the information required for identity appropriation. An alterative to centralized biometric authentication is smart-card based authentication. In this case, the smart card is imprinted with the biometric, so that only the individual who has imprinted the card may use it. The use of a distributed smart-card based infrastructure has a very different recovery and protection profile than a centralized system.

In technical terms, biometrics are weak. The entropy in a biometric identifier is low. Protection is difficult. Biometric data are highly distributed; we inherently share biometric data everywhere. Yet biometric systems can be built centralized; thus increasing the threat of catastrophic failure.

However, biometrics are the only mechanism which link a body to a claim of identity. For that reason, organizations that deal with bodies reasonably advocate for and use biometrics. Fingerprints have proven extremely valuable in law enforcement; and the US Department of Defense maintains DNA records in order to identify remains.

Mainstream Biometrics

While there are many possible biometrics, at least eight mainstream biometric authentication technologies have been deployed or pilot-tested in applications in the public and private sectors:[25] (The leaders are listed as the top four.)

---

[25] For a detailed discussion of these mainstream biometrics, see Jain, Bolle, and Pankanti (1999).

Fingerprint

The fingerprint biometric is an automated, digital version of the old ink-and-paper method used for more than a century for identification, primarily by law enforcement agencies. Users place their finger on a platen for the print to be read. The minutiae are then extracted by the vendor's algorithm, which also makes a fingerprint pattern analysis. Fingerprint template sizes are typically 50 to 1,000 bytes.

Fingerprint biometrics currently have three main application arenas: large-scale Automated Finger Imaging Systems (AFIS) (generally used for law enforcement), fraud prevention in entitlement programs, and physical and computer access.

Iris Scan

Iris scanning measures the iris pattern in the colored part of the eye, although the iris color has nothing to do with the biometric. Iris patterns are formed randomly. As a result, the iris patterns in your left and right eyes are different, and so are the iris patterns of identical twins. Iris scan templates are typically around 256 bytes.

Iris scanning can provide quick authentication for both identification and verification applications because of its large number of degrees of freedom. Current pilot programs and applications include ATMs ("Eye-TMs"), grocery stores (for checking out), and the Charlotte/Douglas International Airport (physical access). During the Winter Olympics in Nagano, Japan, an iris scanning identification system controlled access to the rifles used in the biathlon.

Facial Recognition

Facial recognition records the spatial geometry of distinguishing features of the face. Different vendors use different methods of facial recognition, however, all focus on measures of key features. Facial recognition templates are typically 83 to 1,000 bytes. Facial recognition technologies can encounter performance problems stemming from a number of factors, including uncooperative user behavior and environmental variables such as lighting.

Facial recognition has been used to identify card counters in casinos, shoplifters in stores, criminals in targeted urban areas, and terrorists.

Hand/Finger Geometry

Hand or finger geometry is an automated measurement of many dimensions of the hand and fingers. Neither of these methods takes actual prints of the palm or fingers. Only the spatial geometry is examined as the user puts his hand on the sensor's surface and uses guiding poles between the fingers to properly place the hand and initiate the reading. Hand geometry templates are typically 9 bytes, and finger geometry templates are 20 to 25 bytes. Finger geometry usually measures two or three fingers. During the 1996 Summer Olympics, hand geometry secured the athlete's dormitories at

Georgia Tech. Hand geometry is a well-developed technology that has been thoroughly field-tested and is easily accepted by users.

Voice Recognition

Voice or speaker recognition uses vocal characteristics to identify individuals. It involves their speaking a pass-phrase so that the sample they used when enrolling can match the sample the use at the time of attempted access. A telephone or microphone can serve as a sensor, which makes it a relatively cheap and easily deployable technology.

Voice recognition can be affected by environmental factors, particularly background noise. Additionally, it is unclear whether the technologies actually recognize the voice or just the pronunciation of the pass-phrase (password) used. This technology has been the focus of considerable efforts on the part of the telecommunications industry and NSA, which continue to work on improving reliability.

Retinal Scan

Retinal scans measure the blood vessel patterns in the back of the eye. Retinal scan templates are typically 40 to 96 bytes. Because the retina can change with certain medical conditions, such as pregnancy, high blood pressure, and AIDS, this biometric might have the potential to reveal more information than just an individual's identity.

Because end-users perceive the technology to be somewhat intrusive, retinal scanning has not gained popularity with them. The device shines a light into the eye of a user, who must be standing very still within inches of the device.

Dynamic Signature Verification

Dynamic signature verification is an automated method of examining an individual's signature. This technology examines such dynamics as speed, direction, and pressure of writing; the time that the stylus is in and out of contact with the "paper"; the total time taken to make the signature; and where the stylus is raised from and lowered onto the "paper." Dynamic signature verification templates are typically 50 to 300 bytes.

Keystroke Dynamics

Keystroke dynamics is an automated method of examining an individual's keystrokes on a keyboard. This technology examines such dynamics as speed and pressure, the total time taken to type a particular password, and the time a user takes between hitting certain keys. This technology's algorithms are still being developed to improve robustness and distinctiveness. One potentially useful application that may emerge is computer access, where this biometric could be used to verify the computer user's identity continuously.

Classifying Biometric Applications

Biometric applications may be classified in many different ways. James Wayman of the National Biometric Test Center suggests the following seven categories for classifying biometric applications, explained below.
1. overt or clandestine
2. cooperative or uncooperative
3. habituated or not habituated
4. supervised or unsupervised
5. standard or nonstandard environment
6. closed or open system
7. public or private.

Overt versus clandestine capture of a biometric sample refers to the user's awareness that he is participating in biometric authentication.[26] Facial recognition is an example of a biometric that can be used for clandestine identification of individuals. Most uses of biometrics are overt, because users' active participation improves performance and lowers error rates. Verification applications are nearly always overt.

Cooperative versus uncooperative applications refers to the behavior that is in the best interest of the malicious entity, sometimes called a "wolf" in the biometric literature. Is it in the interest of malicious entities to match or to not match a template in the database? Which is to the benefit of the malicious agent, to re-enroll of additional benefits or to be mis-identified as a legitimate employee? This is important in planning a security system with biometrics because no perfect biometric system exists. Every system can be tricked into falsely not matching one's sample and template-some more easily than others. It is also possible to trick a biometric device into falsely matching a malicious sample against a template, but it could be argued that this requires more work and a sophisticated hacker to make a model of the biometric sample.

In systems that store user information in a database, a malicious entity may try to trick the system into divulging biometric samples or other information. One way to strengthen security in a cooperative application is to require a password or token along with a biometric, so that the attacker must match one specific template and is not allowed to exploit the entire database for his gain.

To gain access to a computer, an attacker would want to be cooperative. To attempt to foil an INS database consisting of illegal border crossing recidivists, an attacker (recidivist) would be uncooperative.

Habituated versus not habituated use of a biometric system refers to how often the users interface with the biometric device. This is significant

---

[26] James Wayman uses the term "covert" instead of "clandestine", making the distinction between "covert" and "overt".

because the user's familiarity with the device affects its performance. Depending on which type of application is chosen, the end-user may need to utilize a biometric that is highly robust. As examples, the use of fingerprints for computer or network access is a habituated use, while the use of fingerprints on a driver's license, which is updated once every several years, is a not habituated use. Even "habituated" applications are "not habituated" during their first week or so of operation or until the users adjust to using the system.

Supervised versus unsupervised applications refer to whether supervision (e.g., a security officer) is a resource available to the end-user's security system. Do users need to be instructed on how to use the device (because the application has many new users or not habituated users) or be supervised to ensure they are being properly sampled (such as border crossing situations that deal with the problem of recidivists or other uncooperative applications)? Or is the application made for increased convenience, such as at an ATM? Routine use of an access system may or may not require supervision. The process of enrollment nearly always requires supervision.

Standard versus nonstandard environments are generally a dichotomy between indoors versus outdoors. A standard environment is optimal for a biometric system and matching performance. A nonstandard environment may present variables that would create false nonmatches. For example, a facial recognition template depends, in part, on the lighting conditions when the "picture" (image) was taken. The variable lighting outdoors can cause false nonmatches. Some indoor situations may also be considered nonstandard environments.

Closed versus open systems refers to the number of uses of the template database, now and in the future. Will the database have a unique use (closed), or will it be used for multiple security measures (open)? Recall the fingerprint example from "Template Management-Storage and Security" for employees to enter a building and log on to their computer network. Should they use separate databases for these different uses, or do they want to risk remotely accessing employee fingerprints for multiple purposes?

Other examples are state driver's licenses and entitlement programs. A state may want to communicate with other states or other programs within the same state to eliminate fraud. This would be an open system, in which standard formats of data and compression would be required to exchange and compare information.

Public or private applications refer to the users and their relationship to system management. Examples of users of public applications include customers and entitlement recipients. Users of private applications include employees of business or government. Both user attitudes toward biometric devices and management's approach vary depending on whether the application is public or private. Once again, user attitudes toward the device will affect the performance of the biometric system.

It should be noted here that performance figures and error rates from vendor testing are unreliable for many reasons. Part of the problem is that determining the distinctiveness of a biometric accurately requires thousands or even millions of people. To acquire samples over any amount of time in any number of contexts from this number of people would be impossible. To test for the many variables in each type of application would be impossible in most cases, and too costly in the few where it is possible. Operational and pilot testing is the only reasonable method to test a system. Additionally, vendor and scientific laboratory testing generally present only the easiest deployment scenario of a biometric application: overt, cooperative, habituated, supervised, standard, closed, and private.

Salient Characteristics of Biometrics

The table below compares the eight mainstream biometrics in terms of a number of characteristics.[27]

The first of the four characteristics are if the technology is suitable for verification as well as identification.

The second characteristic is the measure of change in the biometric, e.g. robustness.

The third characteristic is if the biometrics themselves are distinction; and the fourth is how intrusive a direct interaction is required.

As the industry is still working to establish comprehensive standards and the technology is changing rapidly, however, it is difficult to make assessments with which everyone would agree. The table represents an assessment based on discussions with technologists, vendors, and program managers.

Half the systems in the table below can be used for either identification or verification, while the rest can be used only for verification. In particular, hand geometry has been used only for verification applications, such as physical access control and time and attendance verification. In addition, voice recognition, because of the need for enrollment and matching using a pass-phrase, is typically used for verification only.

---

[27] The authors compiled this table from various sources at the SJB Biometrics 99 Workshop, November 9-11, 1999, including Hawkes and Hefferman (1999). See also Jain, Bolle, and Pankanti (1998).

Biometric	Identify or Verify	Robust	Distinctive	Intrusive
Fingerprint	Either	High to Moderate[28]	High	Touching
Hand/Finger Geometry	Verify	Moderate	Low	Touching
Facial Recognition	Either	Moderate	Moderate	12+ inches
Voice Recognition	Verify	Low	Moderate	Remote
Iris Scan	Either	High	High	12+ inches
Retinal Scan	Either	High	High	1-2 inches
Dynamic Signature Verification	Verify	Low	Low	Touching
Keystroke Dynamics	Verify	Low	Low	Touching

Table: Comparison of Mainstream Biometrics

Robustness and distinctiveness vary considerably. Fingerprinting is moderately robust, and, although it is distinctive, a small percentage of the population has unusable prints, usually because of age, genetics, injury, occupation, exposure to chemicals, or other occupational hazards. Hand/finger geometry is moderate on the distinctiveness scale, but it is not very robust, while facial recognition is neither highly robust nor distinctive. As for voice recognition, assuming the voice and not the pronunciation is what is being measured, this biometric is moderately robust and distinctive. Iris scans are both highly robust (because they are not highly susceptible to day-to-day changes or damage) and distinctive (because they are randomly formed). Retinal scans are fairly robust and very distinctive. Finally, neither

---

[28] This is a function of the population using the system.

dynamic signature verification nor keystroke dynamics are particularly robust or distinctive.

As the table shows, the biometrics vary in terms of how intrusive they are, ranging from those biometrics that require touching to others that can recognize an individual from a distance.

Biometric Conclusions

Where previous evaluations identified temporal and pose variations as two key areas for future research in face recognition, the FRVT 2000 showed that progress had been made with respect to the former, but developing algorithms that can handle a year or more variation between image capture is still a very imperative research area. In addition, developing algorithms that can compensate for pose, illumination, and distance changes were noted as other areas of needed research. Differences in expression and media storage do not appear to be issues for commercial algorithms.

The FRVT 2000 experiments on compression confirm previous findings that moderate levels of compression do not adversely affect performance. Resolution experiments find that moderately decreasing the resolution can slightly improve performance, which is good news since many video surveillance cameras do not acquire high quality images - especially aged cameras. In most cases, compression and reducing resolution are low pass filters, and suggest that such filtering can increase performance. [29]

---

[29] Although not covered here, vendors, city governments, and airports have conducted scenario evaluations of face recognition systems to determine their efficacy in specific locations when used by the general population or the airport employees. Overall, these pilots have shown very poor performance.

13. Reputation

All the identity technologies discussed previously assume you exist in some hierarchy. In fact, there are many hierarchies. Yet there are more social networks than hierarchies. Even within a hierarchy there can be putative authorities that are subservient to social networks. The classic example of this is the new minister in the established church. The minister leads the flock, but every party is aware that the established families determine if the flock follows.

Social identities online may exist simultaneously and exclusively. My role as a good neighbor is something of which I am proud, yet it can only be authenticated by my neighbors. The State of Indiana can authenticate my ownership of my home; but cannot comment on my quality as a neighbor. Yet my classification as a decent neighbor, who brings by cookies and invites everyone over for an annual party, is not something that can be centrally authenticated. My relative success in the endeavor of building a social network is a function of the community of neighbors. This community is disinterested in my reputation among my academic peers.

Similarly my standing in the academy is a function of the respect of my peers. Every workplace has some combination of hierarchy of official power and social awareness of competence.

Proving Identity Through Social Networks

Social networks are powerful tool and can be used to enrich the online experience. Social networks can be used to create reputations. Reputations can be used to authenticate specific attributes or credentials.

Referrals made through an existing social network, such as friends or family, "are the primary means of disseminating market information when the services are particularly complex and difficult to evaluate … this implies that if one gets positive word-of-mouth referrals on e-commerce from a person with strong personal ties, the consumer may establish higher levels of initial trust in e-commerce" (Granovetter, 2004). In 2001, PEW found that 56% of people surveyed said they email a family member or friend for advice (PEW 2002b).

Several commercial websites, such as Overstock.com and Netflix.com, utilize social networking and reputations. These sites have created mechanisms to enable users to share opinions, merchandise lists, and rating information. Using these mechanisms, Overstock.com attracted more than 25,000 listings in six months after the implementation of a friends list.

Public forums (perhaps on the vendor's site) and rating systems provide a natural incentive for merchants to act in an honorable manner or otherwise face economic and social consequences. The cost is greater if the sources of the reputation information are trusted. The opportunity for retaliation (through ratings or direct punishment) is an important predictor of behavior in repeated trust games, so venues where merchants cannot "punish" customers have advantages.

As has been demonstrated by game theoretic experiments, data provided from the FTC (FTC, 2005) and PEW (PEW 2002b) social constraints do not by any means guarantee trustworthy behavior. Yet reputations can be used to authenticate (sometimes weakly) specific practices or characteristics. Today reputation systems are used to support evaluation of vendors, users, products and web sites.

Reputation systems attempt to enforce cooperative behavior through explicit ratings. However the design of the reputation system is not trivial. If the reputation system itself is flawed it might inadvertently promote opportunistic behavior. Consider the case of cumulative ratings, as on eBay. On eBay, a vendor who has more than 13 transactions but cheats 25% of the time will have a higher rating than a vendor who has had only ten honest transactions. Vendors game the system by refusing to rate customers until the vendors themselves are rated, thus having the implicit threat of retaliation.

Reputation systems may be centralized, with a single authority ensuring the validity of the reputation, as with eBay. Reputation systems may be distributed, with multiple parties sharing their own reputation information. Like other identity systems, reputations provide weak or strong authentication. Reputation systems may be dedicated (e.g., eBay) or widely utilized (e.g., credit scores).

Reputation systems are community centered or peer produced identity systems. These systems are the result of the merger of two distinct computing traditions: the scientific and the corporate. The most common form of description of these systems is peer production or P2P. The more recent, and more broadly applicable description is peer production. Peer production includes blogs, file sharing, massively parallel community processing, and gaming.

People can come together and do amazing things with no centralized identifying authority. Reputation systems allow individuals to build verifiable records of reliable and trustworthy behavior over time. The American credit rating is an example of a hieratical reputation system. The reputation of who is reliable in a pinch exists in every community. If you recall the opening chapter, identities were all once community-based. In general, community-based reputation failed to scale in the industrial revolution. The connectivity and communications of the information revolution enables utilizing the wisdom of neighbors.

Many technologies are presented as if centralized attribute authentication were the only option. However, social networks can be used to verify claims of attributes ranging from identity to reliability.

In the history of the network, computation has cycled, from distributed on the desktop to concentrated in one centralized location. Peer production systems are at the decentralized end of the continuum. P2P systems utilize the processing power or data storage capacities at the end points of the Internet.

The fundamental basis of P2P is cooperation. Therefore P2P systems require trust, and are an excellent example of reputation. P2P systems also require some level of social trust, because the Recording Industry Association of America has a policy of policing unlicensed music downloading through lawsuits.

P2P systems are fundamentally about sharing resources. Cooperation is required to share any resource, whether it is two children splitting chocolate cake or two million people sharing files. Peer production through P2P therefore requires some degree of trust and security.

P2P systems are powerful because they are able to leverage computers that are not consistently identified by domain name or IP address; and are not always connected to the network. Peer production can leverage machines that have highly variable processing power, and are not designed to have particular server capabilities other than that provided by the peering network. The systems are built to withstand high uncertainty and therefore can accept contributions from anyone with even a modem.

After considering the generic issues of P2P systems, specific systems are described: Napster, SETI @home, Gnutella, Freenet, Publius, Kazaa and Free Haven. Limewire and Morpheus are implementations of Gnutella. These specific systems are used to illustrate problems of coordination and trust. Coordination includes naming and searching. Trust includes security, privacy, and accountability. (Camp, 2001)

These systems provide different examples of accountability through identity or credential management. The range of systems includes both the centralized and the decentralized. Some carefully authenticate results (e.g., SETI @home) and others weakly authenticate. All have dedicated reputation systems; which are not portable between systems.

Functions and Authentication in P2P Systems

The essence of P2P systems is the coordination of those with fewer, uncertain resources. Enabling any party to contribute means removing requirements for bandwidth and domain name consistency. The relaxation of these requirements for contributors increases the pool of possible contributors by orders of magnitude. In previous systems sharing was enabled by the certainty provided by technical expertise of the user (in science) or administrative support and control (in the corporation). P2P software makes end-user cooperation feasible for all by simplification of the user interface.

PCs have gained power dramatically, yet most of that power remains unused. While any state of the art PC purchased in the last five years has the power to be a web server, few have the software installed. Despite the affordable migration to the desktop, there has remained a critical need to provide coordinated repositories of services and information.

Peer production is a decentralized model of processing and resource sharing. Peer production mechanisms provide different functions, and each function requires its own type of authentication. The series of examples that follow connect the function of the peer production system with the associated enabling authentication and identification. The systems vary from centralized and strong to weak and decentralized. All the systems use unique dedicated reputation mechanisms, tailored to the specific function of the system.

There are three fundamental resources on the network: processing power, storage capacity, and communications capacity. All of these are shared without centralized authentication and policing. In fact, resources are shared despite centralized resources focusing on the prevention of resource (e.g., music and video) sharing. All of these require some sort of trust, and thus some authentication. However, the authentication may be of results, reputation of a particular computer, or reliability of a node. P2P systems rarely depend upon identity. Yet these systems manage to perform all the functions expected of the networked system.

Peer production systems function to share processing power and storage capacity. Different systems address communications capacity in different ways, but each attempts to connect a request and a resource in the most efficient manner possible.

There are systems to allow end users share files and to share processing power. Yet none of these systems has spread as effectively as have peer production systems. All of these systems solve the same problems as P2P systems: naming, coordination, and trust.

P2P systems created reputation-based widely distributed mechanisms for peer production. Reputation, in this domain, is broadly construed.

Mass Storage

As the sheer amount of digitized information increases, the need for distributed storage and search increases as well. Some P2P systems enable sharing of material on distributed machines. These systems include Kazaa, Publius, Free Haven, and Gnutella. (Limewire and Morpheus are Gnutella clients.)

The Web enables publication and sharing of disk space. The design goal of the web was to enable sharing of documents across platforms and machines within the high-energy physics community. When accessing a web page a user requests material on the server. The Web enables sharing, but does not implement searching and depends on DNS for naming. As originally designed the Web was a P2P technology. The creation of the browser at the University of Illinois Urbana-Champaign opened the Web to millions by providing an easy to use graphical interface. Yet the dependence of the Web on the DNS prevents the majority of users from publishing on the web. Note the distinction between the name space, the structure, and the server as constraints.

The design of the hypertext transport protocol does not prevent publication by an average user. The server software is not particularly complex. If fact, the server software is built into Macintosh OS X. The constraints from the DNS prevent widespread publication on the Web. Despite the limits on the namespace, the Web is the most powerful mechanism for sharing content used today. The Web allows users to share files of arbitrary types using arbitrary protocols. Napster enabled the sharing of music. Morpheus enables the sharing of files without constraining the size. Yet neither of these allows the introduction of a new protocol in the manner of http.

The Web was built in response to the failures of distributed file systems. Distributed file systems include the network file system, the Andrew file system, and are related to groupware. Lotus Notes is an example of popular groupware. Each of these systems shares the same critical difficulty – administrative coordination is required.

Massively Parallel Computing

In addition to sharing storage P2P systems can also share processing power. Examples of systems that share processing power are Kazaa and SETI @home. Despite the difference in platform, organization, and security, the naming and organization questions are similar in clustered and peering systems.

There are mechanisms to share processing power other than P2P systems. Such systems run only on Unix variants, depend on domain names, or are designed for use only within a single administrative domain. Meta-computing and clustering are two approaches to sharing processing power. Clustering and meta-computing systems, in general, rely on centralized mechanisms for authentication.

Examples of Community-Centric Systems

In this section the general principles described above are discussed with respect to each system. For each system the discussion of design goals, and organization (including centralization) are discussed. Mechanisms for trust and accountability in each system are described.

Given the existence of a central server there are some categorizations that place SETI @home and Napster outside of the set of P2P systems. They are included here for two reasons. First for theoretical reasons, both of theses systems are P2P in that they have their own name spaces and utilize heterogeneous systems across administrative domains in cooperative resource sharing. Second, any definition that is so constrained as to reject the two systems that essentially began the peer production revolution may be theoretically interesting but is clearly flawed.

P2P systems are characterized by utilization of desktop machines characterized by a lack of domain names, intermittent connectivity, variable connection speeds, and possibly even variable connection points (for laptops, or users with back-up ISPs).

Napster

Napster began as a protocol, evolved to a web site, became a business with an advertising-driven value of millions, and is now a wholly owned subsidy of Bertelsmann Entertainment. Yet the initial design goal was neither to challenge copyright law nor create a business. The original goal was to enable fans to swap music in an organized manner. Before Napster there were many web sites, ftp sites and chat areas devoted to locating and exchanging music files in the MPEG3 format, yet Napster simplified the location and sharing processes. The goal of Napster was to allow anyone to offer files to others. Thus the clients were servers, and therefore Napster became the first widely known P2P system.

Before Napster sharing music required a server. This required a domain name, and specialized file transfer software or streaming software. The Napster client also allowed users to become servers, and thus peers. The central Napster site coordinated the peers by providing a basic string matching search and the file location. As peers connected Napster to search, the peers also identified the set of songs available for download.

After Napster the client software was installed on the peer machine and contacted napster.com, Napster the protocol then assigned a name to the machine. As the peer began to collect files it might connect from different domains and different IP addresses. Yet whether the machine was connected at home or at work Napster could recognize the machine by its Napster moniker.

Thus Napster solved the search problem by centralization, and the problem of naming by assignment of names distinct from domain names. Napster provided a list of the set of music available at each peer, and a mechanism for introduction in order to initiate file sharing.

When a peer sought to find a file, the peer first searched the list of machines likely to have the file at the central Napster archive. Then the requesting peer selects the most desirable providing peer, based on location, reputation, or some other dimension. The connection for obtaining the file was made from the requesting peer to the providing peer, with no further interaction with the central server. After the initial connection the peer downloads the connection from the chosen source. The chosen source by default also provides a listing of other songs selected by that source.

Accountability issues in Napster are fairly simple. Napster provided a trusted source for the client; therefore downloading the client is not an issue of trust. Of course, the Napster web site itself must be secure. Napster has been subject to attacks by people uploading garbage files but not by people upload malicious files.

In terms of trust, each user downloads from another peer who is part of the same fan community. Grateful Dead fans share music, as do followers of the Dave Matthews Band. Each groups of fans shared music within their communities. It is reasonable to assert that Napster was a set of musical communities, as opposed to a single community of users.

Not only did Napster make sharing of ripped files common; it also created a mechanism for implicitly rating music. Obscure bands that were next to popular materials may be downloaded, heard, and thus advertised when these tunes would not rate radio play. Niches and subcultures could more effectively identify and share preferences, with m embers self-identifying by the music they choose to share.

Reputation in Napster was based on the number, perceived desirability, and availability of music. Like being a good neighbor, reputation was implicit but observable. Yet this weak reputation system initiated a fundamental change in the nature of the music business.

The success of Napster illustrates that even a weak reputation-based credential system can be powerful. Napster's reputation system is an example of weakly authenticated, centralized, and dedicated credentialing information.

Facebook

Facebook is a social networking site, initiated at Harvard and then available to other campuses. Facebook indicates to those who sign up that they are on a campus-like space. Facebook presents, for example, people at Indiana with an Indiana-themed space.

Facebook makes money by harvesting peer-produced information. The flaw of Facebook is that the authentication mechanisms are weak. Specifically, the authentication of the core Facebook credential (association with a university) is weak.

Facebook has a series of privacy-sensitive default questions for its configuration.

The first four questions are relationship status, standards for dating if you are single, gender and sexual orientation. The next information you are invited to fill out includes your religion. Religion may include a large selection of Christian denominations or simply Jewish according to the definitions provided by the Facebook pop-up. After this you are requested to identify the political candidates you support. Increasingly political candidates themselves have Facebook sites in order to identify and connect with a base of supporters on campuses.

These are centralized, unauthenticated, self-asserted credentials. Notice that this information is distinguished from other, personal information.

Facebook identifies this as basic information, as if these attributes were the ones most often shared.

Figure 8: Facebook Basic Information

Facebook creates a space where the attributes most often discussed are those rarely acceptable to ask in person. For religion, politics, and martial status, the basic identity attributes are also exactly those that cannot be determined in a job interview. However, this information is readily available to other Facebook subscribers.

Facebook information is widely available. Anyone with an email address in an .edu domain can obtain a Facebook account. This means that alumni of a university can view Facebook. Also, anyone who is attending any university in any capacity, including retirees at extension schools and hobbyists taking specialized coursework, can obtain a Facebook account. In fact, there are many university email addresses that are public - for example announcement addresses. It is possible to register with Facebook using one of those addresses, and thus registers anonymously. These weakly authenticated credentials in this imaginary world can have real world impacts.

Facebook uses a social networking mechanism to allow individuals to assert connectivity in a community and also relative placement in the social hierarchy. Social networking forms the Facebook reputation system. Those with more "friends" are seen as having more social capital than those with fewer friends. Those active in online groups and with many tagged pictures are perceived as having a higher status. Thus the individuals who join and utilize Facebook perceive that there is a functioning reputation system. However, that reputation system does not provide an additional authority or abilities. The reputation system in Facebook is not used to authenticate identifiers or credentials.

MySpace

MySpace is a centralized corporate system that nonetheless utilizes peer production. The genius of MySpace is that is made peer production easy. The critical flaw is that this peer production uses indirect and weak reputation mechanisms. While MySpace is similar to Facebook, MySpace is more targeted towards high school and middle school students. Facebook targets college students. MySpace indicates when logging on that it is a space for you and your friends.

Unlike Napster, which authenticated only musical taste via tunes offered for download, MySpace and Facebook do appear to be authenticating identity. However, both are based on self-asserted credentials and identification.

In 2006, a reporter for Wired searched MySpace using the databases of registered sexual offenders. He located nearly five hundred identified sexual offenders with MySpace pages. In one case, the offender had multiple links to fourteen-year-old MySpace participants and a space filled with sexual chat. Before Wired ran the article, this particular offender was arrested based on a sting operation. The response by MySpace was to request that the Federal Government require that every sexual offender have a registered email address. (Poulson, 2006)

MySpace would then bear no cost, and no liability. By calling for a government identity system, MySpace is seeking to externalize the cost of risk mitigation. MySpace seeks to transfer the costs to limiting the risk to government, and thus to us all. Notice that MySpace could have implemented exactly the same search as the Wired reporter, but choose not to. MySpace could use its own reputation system and examine behavior to develop a stronger mechanism for preventing the use of its systems by sexual predators. Instead, MySpace would create a system where first sexual offenders, and perhaps eventually everyone, would have to register an email address. This is a classic example of the economics of identity. A centralized identity system paid for by an entity other than MySpace, creating privacy risks for all, would be optimal in terms of MySpace profit.

The current information in MySpace's reputation system can be used to approach the particular threat of sexual predation. However, that reputation system would cost money. It would be isolated to MySpace, so it would not be a very useful reputation system to subvert. Therefore individuals would have little incentive to subvert the system; and the credentials would be of little use for committing identity fraud. MySpace's political call to create special registered addresses for sex offenders creates risks for others and is not as potent as a targeted system. However, the MySpace proposal would reduce risk and responsibility from MySpace.

It would be expensive for MySpace to police its users. Any policing system would have false positives and false negatives. To the extent that all successful detection of predators were published, MySpace would be safer but it may be perceived as more dangerous.

eBay

eBay is a reputation system that is worth real money. As such eBay has been subject to repeated attacks. Some of those things that consumers might consider attacks are note malicious by the standards of eBay and its sellers. (Caulkins, 2001)

eBay has a reputation system that provides unreliably glowing recommendations to eBay merchants. In fact, many customers of eBay are unhappy with some element of the purchase. Telephone surveys of eBay customers have found discontent and disappointment to be as high as thirty percent. Yet the eBay reputation system indicates only a few disappointed customers. This is because the eBay reputation mechanism is designed to reflect well upon eBay and the merchants. It is organized to enforce positive recommendations and acceptance of unreasonable shipping terms on customers. Claims of quality are often misleading. (Jin & Kato, 2005)

eBay is an auction house. After a merchant offers a good for sale, a buyer bids. The winning bidder agrees to purchase the item for a specific amount. The merchant then adds an unconstrained amount for shipping and handling. If the shipping and handling is excessive the buyer has a limited right to withdraw the bid. Mutually agreed upon withdrawal does not constrain the buyer. However, few merchants will agree that their shipping and handling is excessive. For low-value transactions the shipping and handling is often a multiple of the amount of purchase. Buyers are limited in the number of bids that they are allowed to withdraw, and excessive shipping and handling is not one of the accepted reasons for withdrawal.

Search for Intelligent Life in the Universe

SETI @home distributes radio signals from the deep space telescope to home users so that they might assist in the search for intelligent life. The Arecibo telescope sweeps the sky collecting 35Gbyte of data per day. SETI @home is a supercomputer built from potentially untrustworthy peers. SET @home created a reputation system with each machine rather than each individual having an identifier. [30]

While other examples of peer production in this chapter are analogous to customers rating a merchant; SETI @home is analogous to a merchant evaluating customers. In terms of its use of a reputation system, SETI

---

[30] In July 2002 there were updates to the SETI software in Bulgarian, Farsi and Hebrew. For four years the Iranians and Israelis have been cooperating in the Search for Intelligent Life in the universe. There has been no conflict between the peoples of those nations, at least in this domain. It helps that this is a highly specialized endeavor which requires no trust. It requires no shared trust because of the distribution of the processes.

@home is more similar to eBay than Napster. The reputation system is of course dedicated; but it indicates cumulative ratings of past behavior.

To take part in this search, each user first downloads the software for home machine use. After the download the user contacts the SETI @home central server to register as a user and obtain data for analysis. Constantly connected PCs and rarely connected machines can both participate.

There are other projects that search for intelligent life via electromagnetic signals. Other programs are limited by the available computing power. SETI @home allows users to change the nature of the search, enabling examination of data for the weakest signals.

SETI @home is indeed centralized. There are two core elements of the project – the space telescope at Arecibo and the network of machines. Each user is allocated data and implements analysis using the SETI software. After the analysis the user also receives credit for having contributed to the project.

SETI tackles the problem of dynamic naming by giving each machine a time to connect, and a place to connect. The current IP address of the peer participant is recorded in the coordinating database.

SETI @home is P2P because it utilizes the processing power of many desktops, and uses its own naming scheme in order to do so. The amount of data examined by SETI @home is stunning, and far exceeds the processing capacity of any system when the analysis is done on dedicated machines. SETI is running 25% faster in terms of floating point operations per second at 0.4% of the cost than the supercomputer at Sandia National Laboratories. (The cost ratio is .0004). SETI @home has been downloaded to more than 100 countries.

The software performs Fourier transforms – a transformation of frequency data into time data. The reason time data are interesting is that a long constant signal is not expected to be part of the background noise created by the various forces of the universe. So finding a signal that is interesting in the time domain is indicative of intelligent life.

The client software can be downloaded only from SETI @home in order to make certain that the scientific integrity of code is maintained. If different assumptions or granularity are used in different Fourier analyses, the results cannot be reliably compared with other result using original assumptions. Thus even apparently helpful changes to the code may not, in fact, be an improvement.

SETI @home provides trustworthy processing by sending out data to different machines. This addresses both machine failures and malicious attacks. SETI @home has already seen individuals altering data to create false positives. SETI @home sends data to at least two distinct machines, randomly chosen, and compares the results. Given the number of machines this is difficult. Note that this cuts the effective processing rate in half, yielding a cost/processing ratio of 0.002 as opposed to a 0.004. However, the cost per processing operation remains three orders of magnitude lower for SETI @home than for a supercomputer.

SETI @home strongly authenticates the results of processing. SETI @home weakly authenticates the machines, enough to enable strong authentication of results.

SETI @home has also had to digitally sign results to ensure that participants do not send in results multiple times for credit within the SETI @home accounting system. (Since there is no material reward for having a high rating the existence of cheating of this type came as a surprise to the organizers.) SETI @home can provide a monotonically increasing reputation because the reputation is the reward for participation. In addition to having contributions listed from an individual or a group, SETI @home lists those who find any promising anomalies by name.

Cooperative, weakly authenticated resource sharing is being used to create the largest, cheapest super computer on the planet. SETI does not depend upon identity verification, but rather results verification. SETI moves beyond attribute authentication to validate the results, without requiring any other cooperative information. By having a centralized reputation and results authentication mechanism, SETI @home has created a trustworthy supercomputer out of many untrustworthy machines.

Peer Production and Identification

Peer production in the form of reputation enables communities to value the contributions of distinct member. In some situations, this can be all that is exactly as needed: who is a good neighbor? An isolated individual can obtain a very high rating on eBay while remaining invisible to the network of credit-enabled merchants. However, a predator may also have been enabled in his desire to search for children on MySpace.

There are significant research issues with respect to peer produced reputations, including problems of naming, searching, organizing and trusting information. These are the problems of identity. Because peer production systems require downloading and installing code as well as providing others with access to the individual's machine, the problem of trust is particularly acute. The vast majority of users of peer production systems are individuals who lack the expertise to examine code even when the source code can be downloaded and read.

Peer production systems in 2003 were at the same state as the web was in 1995. It is seen as an outlaw or marginal technology. As with the web, open source, and the Internet itself the future of peer production is both in the community and in the enterprise. Peer production in 2007 is now in the same state as e-commerce in 2001: companies are making money and others are starting to look.

Peer production systems bring the naïve user and the Wintel user onto the Internet as full participants. By vastly simplifying the distribution of files, processing power, and search capacity peer production systems offer the ability to solve coordination problems of digital connectivity.

Identity systems can similarly be enabled to allow individual naïve user to authenticate specific attributes without centralized storage.

Peer production can be used to rate merchants, as well as customers. Peer production creates information about social networks, which is useful for price discrimination. Social networks embed attributes: student, family, member, or professor.

Recall that originally identity was constructed in a community via old-fashioned in-person reputations. The creation of the digital network enables reputation systems to be scaled to serve millions, rather than tens or hundred. Yet reputations thus far have functioned most effectively when they are most targeted.

Scenarios: Four Views of the Future

A scenario is a short creative document that provides a view of an alternate future. Each scenario takes technologies that are available or promised today, and makes assumptions about how these will evolve. Of course, as described above security requires some form of authentication. Authentication requires some identifier. Identifiable data threatens privacy.

Each scenario is a nightmare for at least one group. The single national identifier ideal for efficiency mavens is the privacy advocates' nightmare. The identity theft nightmare offers consolation for no one. Yet complete anonymity can be contrasted with the surveillance society to find out if there is any truly imaginable common ground.

Four of the scenarios offer extreme cases. Yet each scenario should include admiration of potential strengths as well as clear identification of the flaws.

Each of the following scenarios is a story. The choices made on the path may be fanciful or frightening. The point is to identify the extremes, and build to a consensus about what is possible and what is unknown.

Ubiquitous Anonymity: Your Credentials Please

Under this scenario the tools of crypto-anarchy serve the ends of business and e-government. The most effective tools for ensuring anonymity are linked with particular assertions, for example, the assertion of veteran status. Yet financial transactions and information requests can be made entirely anonymously.

Universal National identifier

The idea of a national identifier gained popularity in the United States in the wake of 9/11. The adoption of Real ID makes the construction of national ID as shown in this scenario quite likely, as national identifier program is moving forward through the coordination of the fifty state drivers licenses' authorities. A similar implementation can be seen in some identity management systems, which concentrate all data in a single account. Currently the Social Security Number is widely used as an identifier. This scenario is the equivalent of a single universally recognized "credential."

Sets of Attributes

In this scenario, instead of having only one credential, each person has a set of identifiers stored in secure hardware or in a series of devices. If the single credential is analogous to a signature, then the set of attributes is analogous to the key ring. In this case, the multiple PKIs and devices will have some limited interoperability and potentially complex risk cascading issues. This scenario draws heavily on reputation technologies.

Ubiquitous Identity Theft

This is a world where the information used to prove identity over distance - Social Security Numbers, address, zip code, credit card numbers - are all readily available to identity theft. Driven by the extreme criminalization of sharing copyrighted information, this scenario envisions a future in which identity swapping over the Internet becomes as common as file swapping is today.

14. Scenario I: Your Credentials Please

Paul Syverson

Introduction

Under this scenario the tools of anonymity serve the ends of business and e-government. Service providers can only link transactions to identifiers of individuals when needed for a specific service. These identifiers generally are not linkable to each other: They are service-specific. Most transactions are authorized without the need for even these identifiers by means of anonymous credentials. For example, a person can show that she is authorized for a service as a county resident, or as a veteran, or as disabled, or as having some combination of these without needing to identify herself.

Remote access to services is made over anonymity preserving infrastructures, such as onion routing (Dingledine et al. 2004). Face-to-face transactions are comparable to cash transactions, except that they may be accompanied by some authenticator, for example, presenting a token, knowing a secret, having a personal physical property (biometric), or combinations of these.

The State of Identity

There are many kinds of transactions that can be made more private and anonymous. Most obvious of these are credit transactions. Consider the largest credit transaction that most of us will make in our lives, the purchase of a home.

John buys a house.

John is 30 years old, single, and wants to buy a house. In applying for a mortgage, he presents certificates showing that the same employer has employed him for the last five years. His income has been at least $50,000.00 per year during his employment. He has been renting for the past three years and paying (on time) $1,000.00 per month in rent. No third party can link these facts to each other. However, he can prove that these certificates are all held by the same person and can prove that he is that person. The verifier to whom he has demonstrated that proof can show that he has received such a proof, but cannot reproduce the proof by himself without John's cooperation. Thus, the verifier can show to a third party (such as an auditor) that he has adequately checked John's credentials. Nonetheless, he is not able to take those credentials he has been shown and reproduce the proof itself (so cannot try to pass as John or get credit for John's properties). (Chaum 1985, Brands 2000, Camenisch and Lysyanskaya 2001)

Unfortunately, John has a twin brother who is not as productive a citizen as John. His name is Jim. Jim is no stranger to the court system and in fact has outstanding criminal default warrants against him for not appearing in court. The last time that Jim was arrested he used John's name and social security number because he knew that he was in default and that John had no criminal record. If the local court processed Jim under John's name, he could skip out and John would be left holding the bag.

John has faithfully filed his tax returns for the past five years. This year, as in the past, he is entitled to a state and federal refund. John's state has a law that authorizes the state's department of revenue to hold state tax refunds for scofflaws, those with child support arrearages, and those with outstanding criminal default warrants.

In an earlier decade, Jim's act of unspeakable brotherly love would have succeeded: the court would have issued a default warrant in John's name. When John's bank did a routine credit check on him, the State's lien against his tax refund would pop up. When John went to the local court to clear the matter up, he would be arrested as Jim. The local court would have an imaged picture of Jim on file. Since Jim and John are twins, the imaged photograph of Jim looks like John. John would then be held without bail on the default warrants.

Fortunately John is living in a more enlightened age. As the technology to allow anonymous transactions became more pervasive, society came to realize that authentication is important. Neither the courts nor credit agencies will now respect the sloppy identifiers of an earlier age that could let someone else pass responsibility on to an innocent victim. If John had been living in the first years of the twenty first century, there is a chance that he would have both a credit problem and a criminal record that would lead to his arrest on many occasions, despite carrying documents at all times from his district attorney explaining his circumstances (Sullivan 2003).

Instead, Jim's attempt to claim that he is John is caught by his failure to properly authenticate that he is John. More significantly, the laws and incentive structures have been formed so that any future risk stemming from incorrectly associating John with this arrest would not be his but be born by those elements responsible for the misidentification, such as the credit reporting agencies. Indeed, in this future scenario the restructuring of law and regulation to more properly assign costs will have been as much responsible for the increased attempt to authenticate correctly and assign culpability accordingly as will be the technology that made it possible. (Shostack 2003, Syverson 2003)

Notice that much of the public value of the information is maintained with this scenario. It is still possible to look at the prices of local houses before you buy your own. All the information on property value is readily available here, as it is today. However, the property listings are not longer indexed by ownership.

Fred gets arrested for speeding.

Fred speeds towards Cape Cod and gets stopped by a police officer. The officer checks the history of the car license on the Automobile Police Registry (APR). The register shows the car has not been reported stolen, taken part in any violent crime, or committed unlawful pass on highway tolls. The APR shows information on all types of events linked to the car's current license and that the license is currently attached to the VIN of the car that was stopped, but no information about the car's (current or former) owner. In this scenario, information about EzPass-type mechanisms are linked to the car, but and not its owner. (See Camp and Osorio (2003) for anonymous payment methods.) Any time a person buys a new car, he or she must jointly include the EzPass serial number in the registration of the new car, which gets later updated at the company's database. Additionally, information on the APR cannot be shared with any third party (public or private).

Once the car has been cleared, the officer asks for Fred's driving license and registration. An online check by the arresting officer reveals he has a valid driving license. The driving license is issued by a State agency and provides links to defined biometric characteristics of the license holder, but it does not link to his identifiers in form of name or social security number1. Similarly, Fred is able to show that he is the current registration holder for the car without linking explicitly to other identifiers. There is uniformity of license issuing mechanisms across states. The combination of biometric indicators used in issuing driving licenses cannot be recorded, asked, employed by, or shared to any other public or private entity other than similar driver's database of another state.

Once the validity of the driving license has been assured, the officer checks on the criminal record database for any information associated with that license (speeding, crashes, driving under the influence, etc.). While there is no mention or the identity of the license holder, there is recorded history about previous incidents by each class. In case of speeding, Fred's record shows an entry for the same highway two years ago, of speeding at 80 miles/hour. Today's arrest is included on his record, setting up a warning on it so the license gets yanked if he is caught in one additional speeding infraction. If the police vehicle is offline at the time of the new entry, the record gets queued and gets submitted automatically when online again.

If a person wants to renew a license in the same state, the only changes made are regarding the expiration period and update of biometric indicators. If the person moves to another state, the totality or part of his or her old registry gets downloaded to the new state's database. The difference between the totality or part of the driver's history is made by the differences between legal frameworks of both the old and new state regarding (a) confidentiality of information, and (b) validity and prescription of acts done in places outside the state.

In this scenario, issuing of a driver's license involves a biometric check that no other state has a currently issued driving license to someone with that biometric. However, states' records indicate only whether a license exists and if so what number. This may be checked for redundant assurance at the time of an arrest if the system is online. Otherwise, the relevant data can be briefly stored for check at a later time. Inconsistencies trigger further response. Issuance of new licenses may include transferring of previous driving record to the new license, canceling of a previous license after additional checks that there are no errors about the bearer of the license, etc.

The provision of responsibility and allocation of risk are the critical factors that make this possible. The technologies necessary to make this scenario a reality already exist.

The Path to Today

One available mechanism for anonymity is simply lying about identity, or using shared credentials. For example, bugmenot.com is a web site that provides to those who would rather not be tracked by what they read in the paper shared login identifiers for major news entities and other popular sites. As Bob Blakley has so eloquently put it, "Privacy is the ability to lie about yourself and get away with it." This does not imply a right to lie, but if you can lie about some aspect of yourself and get away with it, then that aspect is effectively private.

Anonymity in the past was also provided to a limited degree because of the lack of ability to link databases with a single identifier. Information was effectively in silos in most cases. Because databases were not linked to each other, there was generally not a way to view all information in a single format. Up until recently, laws concerning privacy and information ownership have been less of an issue because there are bureaucratic and technological hurdles that have limited privacy violations or even enable anonymity.

Payment represents an example of how technology affects anonymity. Thirty years ago, if I wanted to buy a book I would generally walk into a store and pay in cash for that book. The bookstore would know that someone had bought the book, but they would not have the identity of that person, or be able to sell the person's name and preferences. Even if they did keep track of regular customers who willingly gave shipping addresses or gave a phone number to be notified when a book came in, this would be kept locally and in a paper index file. Twenty years ago, I would walk into the store and buy that book with a credit card. The bookstore would know that the book had been purchased, but by keeping track of the credit card numbers, they could also track all the books that I bought and do profiling. Similarly, the credit card company would also know that I had bought a book (or likely had, as the charge had come from a bookstore). Beginning about ten years ago, if I wanted to purchase a book from Amazon, I would create an account to do so. Amazon would know both the books I bought and the information about me: credit card, mailing address, email address, etc. In addition, they kept track of other addresses to which I shipped so would know who my friends and relations were too, unless I took the precaution and inconvenience of shipping everything to myself first.

Amazon knows who I am, because I give up that anonymity for convenience, so they know both the books (and now toys and electronics and clothes...) that I buy and identifiers and other information about me. They have created a single view of two kinds of information about me that had been separate. Previously my anonymity was protected by the division of two pieces of information: my identity and the kinds of things I buy (and for whom, and when, and...). Now, by contrast, a single business has all that information in a single database. One person can easily access a list of all of the books that I have bought, and know quite a lot about my interests, my relations, not just an anonymous number. If in ten or twenty years all of the physical bookstores go away, or cash is no longer accepted at all, then it will become impossible to conveniently and simply make an anonymous purchase of a book.

There are online book merchants that do not require an account to make a purchase. And one can easily make purchases online using single-use credit card numbers---even at Amazon, as I can attest from the many expired numbers it tracks and shows me whenever I make a purchase. While this somewhat reduces my financial risk from exposure of my credit card to the merchant, all other information about me is known, and arranging payment and shipping without revealing significant information about me would be difficult at best. iPrivacy was a company begun at the turn of the millennium that attempted to provide privacy of purchase through the entire process from order, through payment, and even to delivery. iPrivacy was designed to proxy selection, purchase and payment through their system and to use PO boxes for delivery. The consumer still had to largely trust iPrivacy with his personal information and centralized otherwise-separate purchase information at iPrivacy, but it gave the consumer a relatively simple and straightforward means to be anonymous to online merchants in a practical sense. Today, iPrivacy is gone without ever having significant deployment. We can only speculate as to why. They may have failed for any number of reasons not specific to the service they offered. Or it may be that consumers do not pay for privacy unless they can recognize its impact personally and immediately (Shostack 2003).

The Technology and Policies

Laws creating barriers of anonymity are becoming necessary because advances in technology are removing the old barriers of anonymity. Information was too hard to cross-reference in order to violate anonymity. With technology making violations of anonymity ubiquitous, policies are necessary to prevent what the lack of interoperability used to prevent.

Fifty years ago, you went to one doctor and that doctor knew all of your medical issues. Now, people change jobs, insurance companies, etc. with frequency, and their information has to be available for payment as well as treatment. HIPA was instituted in large part because of the vast amounts of information that health care companies hold, but more because of the ease of access and the large number of people with that access. Fifty years ago your family doctor knew all of the same health information that Blue Cross knows now. Additionally, your family doctor knew your identity, as much as Blue Cross does. The new policies become necessary because the information is no longer trusted to a single doctor and receptionist. Given the vast health consortia, information about individuals and their health history is technologically available to far more people than one person could trust (or even know).

Policies need not dictate the handling of personal data per se to have an effect. Laws that first appeared in California and are now being imitated throughout the US require the disclosure of security breaches at a company if personally identifiable information may have been exposed. One impact has been to make privacy risk increasingly visible, widely recognized, and personal as thousands of people are notified after each exposure, and as the media plaster the names of offending companies across the headlines. It may be that iPrivacy was simply ahead of its time. Companies are given a public relations incentive to be more careful with sharing data, more aware of what data they have where and how it is protected, and possibly even what data they bother to collect and store. We cannot yet know whether this will have a significant lasting affect on companies or whether the frequency and size of these breaches will lead to fatalistic complacency.

Closing

This chapter has looked briefly at where anonymity and privacy are today and how they got there. Primarily we have sketched some scenarios of what is possible in a future world where identifiers are generally not needed to make purchases or interact with government service providers and authorities.

Communication and transactional infrastructures are anonymous. This reduces the risk both of privacy and of liability for managing information. If an identifier is required for a transaction it typically need only be pseudonymous, and more importantly, should only come into play someplace removed from the point of transaction. The trend toward trusting every store clerk or online customer-service representative with complete information about you is curtailed. There can still be picture IDs and biometrics that show a person is the owner of a token, and the token can be used in authorizations and the tracking of reputation in various ways. What does not have to happen in this future world is that the "ID" tell the provider of a service who the recipient is.

15. Scenario II: Universal National Identifier

Allan Friedman

Introduction

Fears of terror, the promise of efficiency, and the potential for commercial gain make the prospect of using a single identifier look very attractive. Some believe that every individual in the United States should have a single, unique identifier that is bound to their person by the strength of law, a carefully constructed infrastructure and a robust biometric. The adoption of the Real ID Act and the requirements for RFID in passports indicate a perception of policymakers that identities are too fluid and uncertain.

While expensive and difficult to implement, a universal identifier makes control of personal information much easier, both for governments wishing to provide services and protect citizens, and potentially the individuals themselves trying to control their personal information. But, others note (source) the implementation of a single, unique identifier also can generate dangers for a democratic society including blows to privacy, the erosion of civil liberties, and the strengthening of a central government.

The State of Identity

In the Age of Information, it makes sense to have identifiers that come closer to meeting the needs and potentials of information technology. Thus, each individual is assigned a unique, universal identification number. This aspect, while not trivial, represents only one small part of the identifier challenge; a large infrastructure is necessary to bind the individual to that identifier. This is done in three levels, with increasing security and trust in that binding at each level. This UID serves as a key to access both public and private databases, as well as being the base for security and privacy policies in those databases.

A UID number should not be a secret, any more than a name is a secret. This was one of the great failures of the Social Security number as an identifier: it was widely employed as both an identifier and a verification mechanism. It is unlikely that a stranger will know another's name, and less likely that the stranger will know her UID number. Yet having knowledge of that number should not give the stranger any more power than having a name (and in some cases, less power). The number space should be large enough to avoid redundancy, and ideally leave space for an error bit or other administrative information, yet be small enough to allow an individual to remember the number, if he or she has been prompted for it repeatedly. Alternatively, alphabetic characters could be used to increase the space with fewer digits. This number could be used as a stand-alone for transactions that do not require any large amount of trust. A call to a technical support center, for example, just needs a key to a database so that the technician can pull up the   right   software   specifications   that   an   individual   purchased.

Most transactions, however, require confidence in the participants. Rather than simply knowing what can essentially be treated as public knowledge, a basic level of trust could be conferred on having something. In this case, a smart card is the most likely choice, since it can hold protected information and can be signed by trusted institutions or government agencies for an added degree of security. A swipe of the card could produce an ID number, providing a basic level of verification. More importantly, a swipe could securely reveal to a concerned merchant or government official whether or not an ID holder is a member of a group. Is a consumer in the over-21 group or a traveler in the wanted-for-questioning group? A card reader can send an encrypted query to a trusted database and gain the necessary knowledge, and only the necessary knowledge. This builds a series of protections. A merchant must have appropriate permission to query the database, and each query can be tracked. The cardholder can be more confident that only the necessary information about her is drawn from remote databases, and little personal information actually has to be kept on the card itself.

To fully protect the link between identifier and individual, however, a biometric is necessary. Situations arise where a transaction party may wish to be certain that the person in possession of an ID card is actually the person identified by the card in previous transactions. Essentially, this question is seeking to determine whether the user of the card is the same person who has used the card all of the previous times. This can be asserted recursively with a biometric enrollment on issuance of the card; occasional matching of the cardholder with the biometric on file will help verify that the original individual-identifier link is still valid. This assumes that a biometric will be stable throughout the course of a lifetime; the UID drafters ultimately chose iris recognition. Biometrics are secured only occasionally, and in accordance with the risks of a mismatched identity and the necessary expenses. Obviously, the harm caused by a minor obtaining cigarettes are not on the same order of magnitude as the harm caused by a house purchased in some one else's name. It may be far too inefficient to check the biometric of every flier all the time. Since immigration and customs already performs a biometric check on entering the country (human assessment of a photo ID), a biometric scan dramatically simplified and improved the process.

No system is perfect, especially not one designed to identify almost 300 million distinct individuals. The world of 2003 absorbed a fair amount of fraud and identity deception; a universal ID system reduces the amount necessary to absorb. Society will never approach "scientifically valid" low rates of error in any scheme. An unchallenged ID record alone is not enough to send some one to jail, or permanently confiscate their property. The UID scheme is also not a cheap system of social organization: it will be expensive. American society was threatened by fraud and terrorism, and chose to adopt the nation-wide identity system.

The Path to Today

The path to a universal identifier was not terribly surprising. In an information age, the United States was a society with terrible information management systems. By relying on inefficient analog-world identifiers such as name or social security numbers, systematic abuse was inevitable. Police might arrest an innocent man based on a shared name with a terror suspect and knowledge of a social security number was seen as proof of identity. Integrated into massive but decentralized databases, this information was often inaccurate, and extremely hard to correct, or even verify with any degree of confidence. Even before the major crises of the beginning of the 21st century, government administrators were working to standardize and secure forms of identification.

Two major social problems focused political attention onto the problem of identification, and began to mobilize popular support for what had been the rather unpopular idea of a universal identifier: terrorism and identity theft.

Motivation: Terror and Fraud

After the tragic attacks of September 11, the United States looked around and saw itself as a society poorly equipped to defend itself against an embedded enemy willing to use suicide bombers and independent terror cells. The knee-jerk response of the Patriot Act raised alarms in countless civil libertarians' minds, but despite a period of calm, failed to prevent a second wave of smaller bombings and sabotage projects. Patriot II was hastily introduced, but its shortcomings were actively debated as a series of trade-offs that simply didn't offer adequate protection. Attacks continued on a smaller scale, striking deep into American life, in malls, sporting events and other public venues. Security experts predicted that the nation would be forced to begin approaching domestic security much like other terror-besieged countries such as Israel, and that we lacked the necessary public infrastructures to protect ourselves. Absent a comprehensive, nation-wide system of identification, the United States government would be forced to track everyone actively. With a robust ID system, it was argued, the average American would be freer of invasive surveillance and it would be harder for the bad guys to hide among the good. Politicians were interested in taking *some* major steps to show that the US government could fight domestic terrorism, and began exploring the idea of UIDs in depth.

At the same time, the criminal impersonation and fraud known as identity theft continued to grow. Lax standards in ID documents and no incentive to coordinate or improve ID verification made it easy to obtain papers "proving" that an individual was really someone else. The increasing number of digital transactions even began to make that step irrelevant, as just a few pieces of information were all one needed to remotely obtain credit, make purchases or even commit crimes in some one else's name. Insecure commercial databases were raided for this express purpose. Too soon, however, what was a crime that one individual committed using the personal information of a handful of helpless victims grew into massive fraud schemes run by organized criminals with vast resources. ID fraud grew by 100% in 2002 and cost an estimated $2.5 billion. Over the next few years, increased criminal activity and more sophisticated exploits caused the problem to grow by an order of magnitude. The financial industry and merchants simply could not continue to absorb these losses. The final blow to the system was a series of lawsuits that finally recognized that the fraud hurt not only financial institutions but also the individuals whose lives were significantly and adversely affected as they found themselves unable to erase the mistake from the myriad of information stockpiles. These decisions identified financial and information institutions who could be targeted for civil suits seeking damages and compensation as vehicles of fraud through negligence, even if they had lost money themselves.

Early Efforts

The initial response to many of these issues was to shore up the current system. The Patriot Act mandated minimum standards of identity verification, but these in turn rested on government-issued ID and flawed data collections. A few pieces of information or illegally obtained papers could be used to obtain legitimate proofs of ID. The process of authentication simply didn't have a source of trust. The same problem existed for a harder-to forge driver's license or a "trusted traveler" program: it was fairly easy to break, and once broken, it was very hard to identify the security breach.

Private sector attempts to normalize their databases also met little success. Credit agencies fought with banks, while the myriad of stakeholders, including insurance firms, hospitals and merchants, all attempted to influence the system to their own advantage whilst shifting liability onto other actors. Even steps as simple as altering the consumer credit system produced attempts to change the business model in the status quo or lock-in proprietary standards and produced long court battles. Privacy advocates saw little good that would come out of an ID system designed to meet the needs of private business and opposed almost all proposals. It looked like the only solution would be a massive nation-wide ID system.

A National ID System

The first consensus was that biometrics had to be involved. A short search yielded the iris scan as the most desirable option. It had the best error rates of anything so far tested and further examination bore this out. It was simple to use, and incredibly difficult to directly deceive. Moreover, it had properties appealing to privacy advocates, who started to recognize that a UID was going to move forward, and wanted a seat at the design table. Iris images are difficult to obtain clandestinely or against the will of the subject: it would be much harder to use this for mass public surveillance. The public however, was not very comfortable—especially at first—with using the eyes as identification. Despite the relatively unobtrusive measurement abilities (one meter, minimal light requirements) there is a general sensitivity to having one's eyes "scanned." This, activists hoped, would limit the number of biometric measurements taken.

Bringing privacy advocates into the design process early was a very sage move from the directors of the program. The Attorney General placed the project under the direction of the Department of Justice, but knew that a larger, more neutral ground was needed for administration, so she tapped the Office of Management and Budget and the General Accounting Office to oversee the development coalition. In addition to bringing in a wide array of e-government experts and technologists, the development team sought insight from a range of private industry experts. The understanding from Day 1 was that this UID would serve both public and private roles, and the public and private sector would need to supervise each other within the constraints of data protection legislation. Privacy activists were brought on board to help increase legitimacy and improve public support for the project.

A major concession the privacy community won was the adoption of a data protection regime. Despite continued resistance to the implementation of data protection legislation for some time, citing the Privacy Act 1976 as sufficient protection, it was finally conceded that much had changed in the ability of organizations to access and disseminate private information since then. In 1976, personal computers were not widespread, the Internet was not invented and the processing power of computers was nothing like as great as it is now. All these issues pointed towards the Privacy Act no longer being sufficient to protect citizens. The PATRIOT Act and the Military

Commissions Act have supplanted the Privacy Act. The Privacy Act remains the single most coherent statement of privacy goals, even if these have been temporarily put aside in the name of terror.

Modeled after the EU Directive and the UK's Data Protection Act 1998, this system ensured that whilst a single identifier would be used to create complete information profiles, individuals would be able to ensure that this information was only used for reasons made explicit by the holders of that information. In this way, all parties were protected, the individual is protected from abuse of their information, and organizations were protected from lawsuits by gaining prior permission from the data subject.

In addition, the holders of personal information were also protected against the devastating lawsuits that continued to emerge from victims of identity theft. In some cases, ongoing class action suits were even settled out of federal coffers, to ensure the support of a few peak associations. A federal guarantee system was set up to cover losses directly attributed to failures in the ID system. In addition to helping secure industry support, it was believed that this provision would require stringent enforcement mechanisms. Commercial interests already operating ethically discovered that there was little that needed to change in their business practices to comply with the legislation and yet discovered that international trade particularly with the EU was considerably enhanced by the introduction of data protection legislation.

Politically, the coalition building was a great success. This success in turn furthered the project, since the sunk costs of actual and political capital investment propelled politicians and private sector firms alike into continuing to pursue the goal of a robust UID.

Phase-in

One of the most difficult aspects of the program was the society-wide adoption. Several test programs were successful, if a bit hasty. The first nationwide attempt to enroll all federal employees highlighted a few key problems, such as hardware incompatibility and coping with disabilities. However, the detection of several major cases of fraud among Medicare administrators and the capture of a highly-placed intelligence mole were hailed successes attributable to the system, so general population enrollment went forward.

A conveniently timed wave of tragic attacks increased America's patience with the inconvenience of enrolling. The few stories of Midwestern grandmothers being unable to prove who they were made national press, but were countered with examples of how several terror attacks might have been prevented. A 5 year time line was established, with a sixth "grace year" to accommodate latecomers. Meanwhile, biometric readings were integrated into both the child-immunization and immigration processes and a new generation of Americans came into this country already identifiable. Local officials received federal grants to aid with enrollment record verification; over 20 people were jailed or deported for attempting to obtain fraudulent breeder documents under the new system, with an undetermined number successfully enrolling in the new system using illegal documents or assumed identity. At the late stage of ID rollout, administrators began to pepper their speeches with phrases like "no system is perfect" and "mistakes will be made". This created a call for the administration to admit its mistakes gracefully but without having to concede to liability or compensation. Opinion polls showed that most Americans understood that the system would not eliminate terrorism, but the majority felt it would go far in fighting terror and crime. Based on these polls and recent attacks, few politicians were willing to take a stand against the UID as it began to be implemented.

From the services side, government offices were the first to be equipped with card readers and biometric scanners, since they were also the first enrolled in the system. Again, bugs were ironed out in this initial national introduction phase: banks soon followed as secure sites for biometric readers while security issues were ironed out. The private sector's desire for a successful program helped head off a few disasters, and delayed over-eager administrators from prematurely implementing key aspects of the system. Finally, more general institutions like hospitals and liquor stores began installing card readers and the occasional iris scanner. The American people remained on the whole a little skittish about use of biometric identification, and cash purchases increased somewhat.

As noted below, digital cash plans, unpopular in the age of ubiquitous credit cards, gained more popularity. A few key court battles determined that for certain purchases like plane tickets or guns, the federal government could require some ID trail. A small industry grew specializing in digital cash that linked to an individual's UID in an encrypted database, and claimed that only a subpoena could force them to divulge the link.

The final challenge was how to allow identity authentication from the home, or any other remote site. Given the sheer number of participants in e-commerce and e-government, this problem demanded a solution. The computing industry was already in the middle of a revolution of its own, as the security and content industries pushed towards trusted computing. A version of Intel's Trusted Computing Platform Architecture (TCPA) was adopted and operating systems were tailored to accommodate secure code and hardware devices on these architectures. (See the appendix.) While commercially available biometric devices remained fairly expensive, the card-readers rapidly became affordable, and were soon adopted as access control devices as well.

The universal ID has been adopted with much less trouble than initially predicted. Mission creep was evident from the early days, an expected result of "Deadbeat Dad Syndrome." Once in place, it was very difficult to argue against applying the power of a UID to some important social problem, such as tracking dead-beat dads. It did make fraud easier to detect across federal databases and private information stores as well. Among other side benefits, a more standardized information system has made government information management not only less prone to error, but far more efficient.

The Technology and the Policy: Privacy Protection

The Supreme Court defined modern privacy rights in *Katz v United States* (1967), where concurring Justice Harlan established the test of "reasonable expectations." Essentially, this case held that actions that are conducted publicly couldn't later be termed "private." There are, however, certain *sanctum sanctorums* where we can act freely without fear of unwarranted government surveillance. While much as been written on the full implications of a reasonable expectation of privacy in a technologically dynamic world, there is no question that popular and legal definitions of what is public and private would dramatically shift under a universal identifying regime. The government has the potential ability to glean information about every transaction using the ID infrastructure. We instead have come to rely on statutory protections of personal data and dignity.

The introduction of data protection legislation as indicated previously was modeled largely on those introduced in the EU during the 1990's and consists of six key tenets.

Personal data shall be processed fairly and lawfully

Personal data shall be obtained for only one or more specified and lawful purposes and shall not be further processed or used beyond that purpose.

Personal data shall be adequate, relevant and not excessive in relation to purpose for which it was collected.

Personal data shall be accurate and up-to-date.

Personal data may only be kept for as long as needed for the purpose collected.

Appropriate technical and organizational measures shall be taken against unauthorized or unlawful processing of personal data and against accidental loss, destruction or damage to personal data.

Further, it was recognized that a key technical protection against a complete erosion of privacy is the division between disparate government databases. Although much has been done to improve the compatibility between databases, they remain in separate jurisdictions with separate rules and no one system contains all the total amount of information. Indeed, the preferred way of accessing information across databases is sending the same signed, Boolean queries to an agency. This drastically reduces the harm a rogue operator can commit by compromising on data access point. Cross-referencing is still possible, and may even be desirable, but it would simply be very expensive to pick up and reorganize government databases again.

Internal politics and jurisdictional issues would also make such a task extremely difficult from a policy perspective.

Nonetheless, we are now more dependent on statutory data protections. Our data and personal information is safeguarded in the private sector by the force of law: and within the public sector by the same standards with caveats where issues of security are predominant. Without such protection commercial actors would otherwise be very tempted to exploit the information that is now in their possession. The introduction of data protection legislation however produced unexpected results in that it removed completely the need for the provision of 'Safe Harbor' in order to conduct trade in personal information between the EU and the US. This reduction in the amount of 'red tape' considerably outweighed the administrative costs of implementation of the data protection legislation, and has increased trade by an order of magnitude that surpasses initial costs of compliance.

As social concerns come to the forefront of the American political scene, the temptation will be strong to rely on personal information in seeking a solution to other social ills, in this way the problems mission creep has become an issue requiring further consideration. On the other hand, in the face of such ubiquitous government information control, the right of citizens to check the reliability and accuracy of the personal information held is of paramount importance. Clearly, any system that contains large amounts of personal information with the intention that it provides government agencies with a source of intelligence, by its nature must ensure its accuracy or risk failure in its application.

There remains however, a general concern about the ease with which one may be monitored. Not surprisingly, much of the discomfort centers on potentially embarrassing behavior that many wish to avoid publicizing. This may involve those who frequent gay bars or the birth control choices of individuals.

After a decade of losing ground to the credit card, cash has seen a mild resurgence. Since use of a credit card almost always is accompanied by an ID card swipe, and the occasional iris scan, this can leave an electronic trail. Despite some legal data protections for UID purchases, the comfort of being as anonymous possible when purchasing a controversial book has led many to pay with cash. Digital cash vending machines add the convenience of plastic to the anonymity of cash, much like a debit card but without traceability. After languishing in the prototype phase for years, several competing companies now offer digital cards that can be loaded with money anonymously, and are accepted wherever credit cards are taken.

The Department of Justice feared that cash purchases might put a stop to exactly the sort of information gathering they hoped to perpetrate under a UID system, and urged Congress to act. A number of suspicion-arousing transactions, from weapons to pornography, were declared to require UID registration. Some of these, such as nitrate fertilizer that can be used to make explosives, were accepted without a fight. Others, particularly those that tread on the toes of proponents of the First and Second Amendments, were challenged in the courts. Data policies were fine-tuned based on specific applications and interest group pressure. The UID could be used for firearms background checks, for instance, but no record of the purchase could be kept in government databases.

Trust and Administration

A key weakness in any secure data system, especially one controlled by the state, is the centralized power of administrators. A system in which administrators have little power is a system that cannot be administered with any degree of efficiency or flexibility. Records will always need to be updated or corrected, added or deleted. Yet if every administrator could interact with the UID system with impunity, fraud would be easy and incredibly hard to detect. The solution, then, is to bring accountability to the administrators by keeping a careful record of each action. If a record is changed, deleted or added, the administrator signs the transaction with his or her information, including jurisdiction or perhaps even his or her own UID. It should be almost impossible to change something without any trace. This protects the system against bad information by error or malice by allowing audits and error checking.

In the event that there is a dispute between what an individual a piece of information in a UID database and the claim of an individual identified by that information, an audit trail should be clearly evident. While all disputes may not be able to be settled in this fashion, a large number of them can be, such as explaining discrepancies between two databases. At very least, it offers a starting point for conflict resolution, even enabling some of the process to be automated.

We can imagine a rather narrow set of constraints under which true identity must be protected for reasons of public interest, such as witness protection, undercover policing or (state) espionage. Not every person with access to auditable records needs to know, or even should know that records have been altered. Still, we can imagine a series of protected files, with some amount of security protection that can be used to record all but the most sensitive of these actions. The ability to make untraceable changes should be guarded as fiercely as possible; allowing only a very few people to have that authorization.

The Future of UID

As the system grows more and more trusted, those with a bolder social agenda have encouraged exploiting a reliable identity system for programs that would otherwise be much less feasible. Some drug reformers, for example, have urged rehabilitation of addicts with some sort of prescription of addictive drugs to avoid the disincentive of cold-turkey withdrawal, a very painful process. While there are many criticisms of such a plan, a major obstacle to implementation is making sure that the drugs go to the addict in treatment and that addict alone. A greater amount of trust in an identification system would make such a system more likely.

The problem with increasing the trust in ID authentication systems is that it increases the incentive to subvert the system. The incentive for fraud is much higher when a valid ID can permit access to more desired goods and services. However, it should be easier to detect those seeking to engage in active fraud, like obtaining government benefits, or claim large sums of money from a bank because of the nature of the biometric on file. The very fact that they are placing themselves into a smaller, select group should make detection less difficult. A UID makes validating a claim of identity easier to the extent that the security of the UID is acceptable to the party asking the identity question. Yet to the extent that it can be abused against the interest of the actual person whose identity is being identified a UID is a threat not a promise.

16. Scenario III: Sets of attributes

Barbara Fox

Introduction

We live in a world where it's impossible to maintain a single identity. Our family, our schools, our friends, our bank, and even our government assign us different roles and titles, which come with different identifying names and numbers. We contribute to the confusion by choosing our own pseudonyms for online transactions. We manage the complexity that comes with this plethora of personal identifiers because we wish to remain in control of our identity.

The perception of being in control drives us to reject a national identity card due to its potential for abuse by privacy-invasive applications from both industry and government, as well as its potential to increase the risk of identity theft. This scenario projects how we will continue to manage our multiple identities as priorities of privacy and security in national consciousness evolve. While we anticipate the potential for law and policy to make grade strides, the unrelenting advance of technology is certain to ensure that will continue to face tough policy questions around our identities in 2014.

The Evolution of Identity

Surprisingly, the average American citizen has only a handful of transactions with his government for which she needs an identifier. Identification cards and numbers are used much more frequently outside our interactions with government. These transactions are described in the following two subsections that describe how identifiers are used in 2040 and how they were used in 2004. Changes center in how government issued IDs may be used by industry and how the firms that collect it may share identifying information. The few changes in the identification infrastructure are highlighted in the following text.

How IDs are used in 2040

In 2002 there were 162,000 reported cases of identity theft, almost double the 86,000 reported the year before. A quarter million cases of fraud resulting from identity theft would be reported in 2003. These doubled again in 2004. (FTC, 2005) In 2006, identity theft insurance, identity theft management, and even advertisements on television addressed this now ubiquitous problem

However, concerns from fraud would be overshadowed that summer when an investigation into a serial rapist led to a Boston pool hall at which each victim's driver's license had been scanned to reveal not only their age, but their name and home address. A search of the perpetrator's apartment revealed lists of purchases made by victims at merchants with which the pool hall shared information. This explained how the perpetrator had found the victim's homes and sent gifts to the victims before each crime, facts that had led investigators to believe that the victims had known their attacker. Extensive press coverage ensured that the consumer backlash not only hit those who collected information, but those who shared it.

In October of 2015, Congress made two unprecedented moves to guarantee individual privacy. It effectively repealed the USA Patriot Act (HR3162) passed in the wake of the September 11, 2001 terrorist attack and extended federal pre-emption of state privacy laws under the Fair Credit Reporting Act, by passing the Consumer Privacy and Safety Act (HR1984). The Act:

1.   Mandated that states either update driver's licenses, or provide additional proof of age identification cards that did not reveal the holder's address.

2.   Made illegal the collecting, selling, purchasing, or other exchange of consumer information without a separate opt-in contract, in a standard format issued by the federal government. Conglomerates faced regulations that limited the consumer information that could be shared across business units.

3.   Mandated that social security numbers could not longer be requested, stored, or exchanged for non-governmental use other than tax accounting.

4.   Mandated that payment and other transaction information could only be shared if the consumer granted permission for each transaction at the time of the transaction. This not only enabled the continuation of frequent flyer and other affinity programs from large firms, but also ensured that small firms could work together to bundle products and verify that products were indeed sold together. This allowed them to continue competing with larger firms that produced the full complement of products.

Critics of the bill argued that consumers in many states lost important privacy protections with its passage. But public response to a single federal agency accountable for every aspect of identity theft management was overwhelmingly positive.

Because of minimal changes with existing governmental IDS, little changed in the way citizens interacted with their government. The most noticeable change was that more technology was introduced into police cars to retrieve driver information that was no longer on licenses from remote sources.

Despite a major outcry from businesses, the majority of changes came in the level of disclosure provided from businesses to customers about information practices. In order to be able to continue to maintain merged records, firms rushed to get consumers to opt-in to existing sharing arrangements. These individual credit availability numbers (or I-CANs) were introduced before the legislation went into effect in late 2005, as a non-governmental identifier to replace the social security number for use in non-government transactions.

I-CANs were the product of an open international competition sponsored by the National Institute of Standards. Some proposals contained only a means for uniquely assigning numbers to individuals, leaving the authentication problem to be solved later. Others proposed detailed specifics of smart-cards designs containing digital signature and encryption technologies that not only enabled identity authentication, but also offered delegation and the ability to audit. The I-CAN authentication problem drove demand for low-cost, easy-to-use secure ``identity storage appliances." These now-ubiquitous devices are easy to connect to personal and public computers. The devices hold a virtually unlimited number of unique identity enablers (private digital signature keys and associated certificates.)

While the final I-CAN standard and the I-CAN program became an unqualified success, it remained completely voluntary and covers only twenty percent of the US population. A full ten years later, the question remained of whether it should be extended, this time at government expense, to I-CAN2.

For practical purposes, the technology issues associated with a national identifier are off the table. I-CAN proved that we have the technology. What we are left with is the more difficult legal and policy questions that plagued us in 2004. Does the promise of digital government demand that we step up to answering them?

17. Scenario IV: Ubiquitous Identity Theft

Ari Schwatz

This scenario offers a view of the world that most observers today would consider a worst case. Identity theft, characterized by law enforcement as the fastest growing crime in the United States, (GAO, 2000) has grown exponentially. Identity theft grew beyond epidemic proportions as confirmed by the Federal Trade Commission. (FTC, 2005) Due to continued weaknesses in identity frameworks, increased demands for information upon using and purchasing content and increased weaknesses in security, it is quite common for individuals to feel comfortable assuming the identity of others simply to protect themselves. For example, the medical database begun under Bush has no meaningful privacy protection. (Pear, 2007) Obtaining care at a pharmacy or minor emergency center that might result in future refusal to insure or personal embarrassment requires a credit card and id in a false name.

Assertions of identity are still utilized for social protocol and historical necessity. Yet the assumptions about individual identity to information links on which so many systems have been built have been broken down. Continuing ad-hoc methods of authentication are attempted, but subverted as soon as they are widely implemented.

The State of Identity

Interacting with the government in a world of ubiquitous identity theft is confusing and frustrating endeavor. Some agencies still have complex authentication, verification and authorization schemes in place that just do not work and burden the process. Other agencies have given up completely, preferring instead to rely on face-to-face transactions. Most service agencies have learned to live with high rates of fraud and exposure of citizen information to snooping.

New laws have been put in place to harshly punish the worst fraud offenders. While the deterrent does not seem to work for small time theft, it has been somewhat effective for large-scale long-term repeat offenders where prosecutors can build up a case. This has relieved enough pressure on the judicial system to make most believe that this is all that can be expected from law alone at this point. Most of the culprits of widespread fraud are beyond the reach of American law, in Nigeria or Eastern Europe. The credit card processing companies have no interest in investing to reduce such fraud, because the investments may cost as much as the fraud. In addition, the cost of much fraud can still be pushed to the consumer through the use of PIN systems as with the United Kingdom.

One example of the repeated failures in authentication systems is the online Personal Earnings Benefit Estimate Statement online at the US Social Security Administration (SSA). Originally, beneficiaries could get an online statement describing working history and long term benefits by filling out a detailed form providing explicit personal information such as mothers maiden name, date of birth and address as listed on their last paycheck. Soon after going online, it was recognized that this information was far too easy for anyone to get. The SSA tightened security by sending a confirmation email message with a password. Soon after this measure went into effect, it became an increasingly easy and common practice for identity thieves to hijack email accounts. Then SSA switched to telephone "call backs" where they would ask "out-of-wallet questions" such as employment history, salary information and more. This process had the down side of being expensive (to pay for call centers) and cumbersome (true beneficiaries often could not answer the out of wallet questions correctly), but it did work for a few years. Eventually, however, even this measure has failed. Insiders in call centers of this kind began to regularly misuse and share the transaction information and it is quite simple and common to set up a phone in another person's name for a short period of time.

RealID was an expensive debacle that increased the flow of citizen information and ease of information theft. Driver's license authorities continue to be valuable sources of false identities, only those now work uniformly across state lines. The rate of identity fraud, and the economic necessity of credentialing illegal immigrants doomed the project from the start.

Other government offices have simply stopped providing services that require authentication. For example, individuals can no longer reserve a campground space in a national park in advance. Secondary markets and the ease of identity fraud caused the cost of popular campsites to skyrocket, and organized crime had become involved. Campsites had to return to first come, first serve.

Obviously many government agencies do not have the ability to reduce services in this way. For example, while most benefit offices have abandoned hope of providing benefits electronically over distances, they still need to provide basic services that require authentication. Beneficiaries are now expected to come into the office where large amounts of biometric data (via photographs and DNA samples) are taken about each visitor. The biometric information does not help in authenticating individuals. Identity thieves were able to duplicate and falsely populate biometric databases long ago. Instead the biometric information is used to help in fraud cases in the new, specially created, district fraud courts used to prosecute egregious offenders.

The Path to Today

How did we get ourselves into such a situation? As we look back at the choices made at the beginning of the 21st Century it seems that the problems we currently encounter were almost unavoidable. Trust in the system at first crumbled on the edges and then a critical mass of failures brought the system down upon itself.

As early as 2001, the US Federal Trade Commission (FTC) was reporting that identity theft was growing at alarming rates, almost doubling every year. (FTC, 2002) Yet, awareness of the problem was not commensurate with its scope and impact. (GAO, 2002) Several factors played critical roles in the slow decay that began in the 20th Century and played it self out in the next. These factors included:

Weaknesses in "Breeder Documents" — Historically, authentication systems relied on a small number of documents used to verify an individual's identity. These documents are often called "breeder documents" because a few of them are used to create all other individual identity credentials and then make it possible for an individual to open banking accounts, establish credit and generally live under a real or assumed identity. (AAMVA, 2002) Yet, as a greater reliance was placed on the small number of breeders not suited for the purpose, problems (previously know and unknown) started to arise. In particular, many problems can be seen with the following breeder documents:

Birth Certificates

The first individual identity document given to people born in the United States is the birth certificate. Many other documents rely upon it. However, since municipalities control the issuance of the certificate, there are literally thousands of issuers with no set security or information standards for the certificate. Identity information often used in later identity authentications is not as helpful at birth as it is with adults since eye and hair color are not set and fingerprint ridges are too close together to read. Also, many individuals are not born in hospitals, making verification of individuals at birth very difficult for the localities. Finally, early implementations of biometrics stored raw biometric data, so the affluent early adopters have completely lost control of their own information. The documents have been easy to forge and localities have had no incentives to continue maintaining a relationship with the holder of the birth certificate making databases of current information practically useless. (CSTB, 2003)

Social Security Numbers (SSN)

The SSN was created in 1936 as a means to track workers' earnings and eligibility for Social Security benefits. Although the number was not originally intended to be a National ID number, it has been used for almost every imaginable purpose. The Privacy Act of 1974 was written, in part, to cut down on the federal government's reliance on the SSN, yet it has not stopped most uses. Meanwhile, use of the SSN by state governments and the private sector has continued to grow. Aside from the fact that the number was not properly designed to be used as an authenticator for such varied purposes. The overuse and public use of SSNs have made the numbers widely susceptible to fraud. Since the Social Security Administration is not generally in the business of verifying SSNs for the private sector criminals have made up plausible nine digit numbers or, more frequently, begun using a real person's SSN.

Driver's Licenses

While driver's licenses were created for the purpose of insuring safety on state roads, the license has become a de facto photo government issued identification card. Yet, the system is clearly not designed to issue universal photo identification for multiple reasons:

Since the driver's license is not given to someone at birth and non-US born individuals must also be allowed to obtain a license, the state issuer must rely on a series of other documents to authenticate the individual.

The authorities providing driver's licenses serve drivers and non-drivers, citizens, legal residents, and temporary visa holders so there are many issuers within a state, putting strain on communications and weakening security. The desire for service prevents a high degree of verification.

Employees are underpaid, disrespected, and overworked creating an atmosphere ripe for high levels of bribery and corruption.

States have various physical security concerns including a number of break-ins where computers and blank cards were stolen to make fake cards.

If the value of a driver's license is as high as the value of American citizenship, the cost of fraud prevention is not as high as the market value for a fraudulent license.

These problems and others led to a system where fake cards and falsely issued driver's licenses are common. As early as 1999, it was estimated that California alone wrongly issued 100,000 per year. (LoPucki, 2001; Schwartz, 2002) By 2003, corruption was so rampant in New Jersey that the DMV fired the entire staff of the Newark branch office. (CDT, 2003)

Generally speaking, the agencies distributing breeder documents have little investment in their secondary use. By the time the agencies themselves were implicated, they were unable to stem the tide of use of the documents for authorization, marketing and other purposes.

The Growth of Identity Card Information "Swiping" — Continued use of information storage on the magnetic stripe of cards and the low cost of portable magnetic stripe readers led to a rampant increase in the theft of personal information directly from identification cards. In early 2003, only identity thieves and a few rogue businesses (bars and clubs) were using readers, but their popularity grew quickly and fair information practices were ignored. Calls for legislation to prohibit the practice went unheeded and collecting information off of cards for legal and illegal uses became routine.

Another driver to the world of ubiquitous identity theft was the lack of a coherent public records policy. The advent of networked technology brought the knowledge that an individual's life, activities, and personal characteristics can be found scattered throughout the files of government agencies. Companies quickly constructed detailed profile of an individual using only publicly available, individually identifiable information from government records. As more of this information became available in electronic form, individuals began skipping the information aggregators and building their own profile database of friends, neighbors and others.

While the types of records available from jurisdictions may vary, the information available on a given individual (and a likely source of the information) can include:

- Name and address (drivers license)
- Social Security Number (driver's license number in some states)
- Home ownership (land title)
- Home loan (land title)
- Assessed value of home (property tax)
- Size of home, price, physical description (land)
- Parents (vital statistics)
- Sex (drivers license; vital statistics)
- Date of birth (drivers license; vital statistics)
- Selected occupations (occupational licenses)
- Voting frequency (voter registration)
- Political Party
- Political contributions (Federal Election Commission)
- Selected hobbies (hunting/fishing licenses; town web site access)
- Boat/Airplane ownership (license)

Court records detail much more information. In particular, companies routinely collect the information of individuals who has interacted with the courts as a criminal defendant, as a plaintiff or defendant in civil litigation, as a juror, through divorce proceedings, in bankruptcy proceedings, as a beneficiary of a will, or in other ways through court records. Additional information is also available about individuals who are required to file information on stock ownership with the Securities and Exchange Commission; political candidates and government employees required to file ethics disclosure forms with state or federal offices; recipients of student loans, housing loans, small business loans, and other forms of government assistance; and employees who have filed workers compensation claims.

Information on the driver's license was forbidden to be shared by the Driver's Privacy Protection Act in the late '90s, yet some states continued to push the limits of the distribution of information, selling information to private data marketers. (AP, 2003) This information includes:

- Make and model of automobile owned (motor vehicle)

- Automobile loans (motor vehicle)

- Driving record (drivers license)

- Selected medical conditions (drivers license)

- Social Security Number (drivers license)

- Height and weight (drivers license)

As public information was made more available in electronic form, concurrent with the advent of intelligent search tools made all of this information easier to sort through, data aggregators were no longer needed and individuals began to build their own databases on friends, colleagues, neighbors and others.

A Lack of Incentives to Fix the Problem in the Marketplace

As the costs to society of greater identity theft began to increase, so did the cost to business, yet not enough for companies to take actions to stem the problem.

By 2002, cases involving thousands of victims were becoming routine with insider fraud and poor security at financial and medical companies the main culprit.[31] On a smaller scale, many major financial institutions were routinely giving out confidential customer account information to callers, using security procedures that authorities said, even at the time, were vulnerable to abuse by fraud artists. (O'Harrow, 2001)

A report issued by the Tower Group in 2002 estimated that identity theft cost companies at least $1 billion in fraud. The report claimed that banks had no means to positively identify individuals. Yet banks and other companies were simply unwilling to spend money on possible preventive resources for such a complex problem.

Privacy Protections Did Not Keep up with Technology

The legal framework in the United States did not envision the pervasive role information technology would play in our daily lives. Nor did

---

[31] In November 2002, a Massive identity theft ring broken up misusing Ford Motor Credit credentials, with 30,000 victims. In December, theft of medical information on 500,000 military-related from TriWest Healthcare Alliance on 14 Dec 2002 See Peter Neuman's Risk Report for these and other examples.
http://www.csl.sri.com/users/neumann/illustrative.html#33

it envision a world where the private sector would collect and use information at the level it does today. The legal framework for protecting individual privacy reflects "the technical and social givens of specific moments in history." (Sullivan, 2003) A relevant example — the Privacy Act, passed in 1974, covers only groups of any records "under the control of any agency from which information is retrieved by the name of the individual or by some identifying number, symbol, or other identifying particular assigned to the individual." Yet the law does not take into account the fact that an agency may be collecting information in a distributed database that is not currently retrieving information by an identifier. It also does not address protections for government subscription services to information brokers that are maintained by the private sector. (Mulligan, 1999; Schwartz, 2000)

Vestiges of a pre-Internet, pre-networked world, stressed the privacy framework. Foremost among these was a belief that the government's collection and use of information about individuals' activities and communications was the only threat to individual privacy. Exacerbating this was the antiquated notion that a solid wall separated the data held by the private and public sector; and that the Internet would be used primarily for a narrow slice of activities. Finally there was a presumption that private and public digital networked "spaces" were easily demarcated.

Creating privacy protections in the electronic realm has always been a complex endeavor. It requires an awareness of not only changes in technology, but also changes in how citizens use the technology, and how those changes are pushing at the edges of existing laws and policies. While there were several pushes for a comprehensive privacy law, such a law never took hold.

Requirements of identity for copyright purposes became routine as liability law continued to shield providers of flawed technology creating a vacuum of responsibility - Bolstered by court rulings such as RIAA v. Verizon,[32] intellectual property holders pressured companies to identify users of content. Rather than fight, ISPs and software companies began allowing anyone with an intellectual property claim to request identity information from users. Meanwhile, the constraints on security research embodied in the DMCA allowed providers of identity systems (Netiquette, Sun, and multiple start-ups) to hide the security flaws. Finally Microsoft required compliance with its own single sign-on standards to access any Web Server using NT. Combining a situation where individuals had to turn over personal information for every transaction online with the systemic security flaws in the single sign on, identity became liquid and readily available to almost anyone online.

---

[32] The most relevant opinion, RIAA v. Verizon opinion can be found at http://www.dcd.uscourts.gov/03-ms-0040.pdf. Please also see CDT's statement on the case http://www.cdt.org/copyright/030130cdt.shtml.

A policy focus on identity theft came, but far too late in the spread of the problem. The focus was also not on restructuring the root causes of the theft, but on criminal penalties and awareness. Since it takes individuals 14 months on average to determine that their identity has been stolen, outrage always lagged behind action. (GAO, 2002)

Eventually, identity theft grew from a problem where everyone knew a victim to one where everyone was a victim, multiple times over. The way to fight back was not to report the crime, but to steal someone else's identity instead. Corporate practices of requiring identification to purchase a CD; requiring information for every use of payment instruments; and increasing interruption-based marketing left consumers with little capacity to protect their privacy. The systems meant to prevent consumers from providing misinformation to marketers instead drove otherwise law-abiding people into identity thieves. The distinction between the criminal and common was the purpose and extent of use.

18. Closing

The four scenarios show that there are really only two choices: decentralized, often anonymous credentials or ubiquitous identity theft. Within the range of reasonable anonymity there are different choices for breeder, foundational documents. The question is "who are you" in a social paper world becomes "what are your credentials" in a digital networked world but rather. Confusing those questions will create another generation of identity theft with the same convenience of easy credit at the same costs in broken records and hindered lives.

The question of who you are is profoundly distinct from the question of the identifiers you may require. The confusion between these two basic ideas, identity versus credentials, creates very real risks. The question of who you are is not distinct from the risks you already face from a chronically inadequate identity system.

What problem are corporate and national identifiers supposed to solve? What new problems will the new identity systems create? Considering identity management more broadly, it is possible to conceive of an environment where there is one central key? What myriad of keys will be needed for the different identity puzzles? Each of the systems above has strengths, and none is appropriate for all environments.

Today we are headed more to the last scenario than any other. Surveillance for terror, crime, money and copyright policing is exploding. A study of home wireless use of students at IU found that a year of intensive education reduced rather than increased use of security mechanisms for student home wireless systems. Security seemed to be authority, offering the students only non-repudiation.

Even a theoretically technically perfect identity system will create new problems, particularly to the extent that it fails by design to solve a specified unique problem. Each system, even in the few above, has very different failures and strengths. Biometrics are incomparable at preventing duplicate enrollment. Biometrics are fundamentally flawed at verification of unique identity over a network. Card Space is decentralized, but may not be fully documented. Liberty Alliance is fundamentally an enabler of corporate data sharing. Reputation systems can be strong in cryptographic terms, but the distribution of enrollment responsibility means that they are inherently weak in organizational terms.

Identity management is not magic. With millions of people on the Internet, no one can know who each one is. Criminals already have anonymity through identity theft, botnets, and fraud. In pursuing these malicious few, identity systems are both removing autonomy from the innocent and ironically creating ever more opportunities for the malicious.

Generic identity architectures are being built with so many purposes as to have no functional purpose in terms of security; but are highly effective at violating privacy. Privacy plus security is not a zero sum equation. Just as no structure would be an ideal home, a perfect school, and an optimal office, no single identity structure will address identification of duplicate enrollment for fraud, distinguishing age, verification of financial status, graceful degradation, seamless recovery, and optimal availability. A set of distributed systems, that are purpose-driven rather than ubiquitous, with the strongest appropriate authentication offers the best potential for being supple enough to allow society and designers to recover from our inevitable mistakes.

These are risks for the future. Today, identity is simply used to shift risks. New modes of interaction are clearly needed. We are replacing implicit human identification with explicit inhuman identity management. This has proven inadequate.

Current identity systems are designed to increase the concentration of data and minimize the liability of the purveyors of those systems. From Yahoo! providing the name of a Chinese blogger to Amazon experiments with variable pricing, liability is being paced on those with the least control. Identity systems violate privacy in order to increase the profits of the corporate or national entities paying for the ID systems. Without privacy controls, we all lose.

At the level of the implementing software, each person entrusts critical information to software providers. Yet, why trust e software providers when they have proven trustworthy. Today, providers of software have escaped even the minimal common law requirements for selling a functional good as promised. Yet these good are sold with exploitive end user license agreements.

Education has been presented as the solution to everything from computer crime to identity theft. Yet the asymmetry in power means the customer can do little about identify theft. Educating the consumer can do little when the consumer is structurally helpless.

Until the discussion of identity management is expanded to include anonymity management, forward movement is limited. Spam is a good example of a difficult identity problem. Spam is not one problem; it ranges from the level of theft equivalent to stealing a donut from the office lounge to Enron levels of international criminal fraud.

Identification without anonymity is neither reliable, nor desirable. Online identity is inherently an oxymoron. Our identities, which we are, are part of the physical world. Credentials are digital; people are not. Until there is considerably less money to be made off the illusion that we can be represented with perfection online, that fiction will continue to endanger our finances, our reputations, and even our freedom.

19. References and Further Reading

Abric, J.C & J.P. Kahan (1972), "The effects of representations and behavior in experimental games", *European Journal of Social Psychology*, Vol 2, pp 129-144.

Akerlof, G. A. (1970), "The Market for Lemons: Quality Uncertainty and the Market Mechanism", *Quarterly Journal of Economics*. 84:488-500.

Anderson, R. (1994), "Why cryptosystems fail", *Comm. of the ACM*, v. 37, n. 11, Nov., pp. 32-40.

Anderson, R. (2002), "Unsettling Parallels Between Security and the Environment", *Workshop on Economics and Information Security*, Berkeley, CA.

Associated Press (2003) "ACLU Says Florida Illegally Sells Driver Records to Companies," *Sun Sentinel*, April 9, 2003.

American Association of Motor Vehicle Administrators, (2002) "Fighting Fraud: One Document at a Time," *Move Magazine*, Winter 2002.

Avery, C & P. Resnick & R. Zeckhauser (1999), "The Market for Evaluations", *American Economic Review* 89(3): 564-584.

Axelrod, R. (1984), *The Evolution of Cooperation*. New York: Basic Books.

BBC, 2004 "Doctor Acquitted of Porn Charges", 21 April 2004, available at: http://news.bbc.co.uk/2/hi/uk_news/england/humber/3647207.stm

Barney, J. & M. Hansen & B. Klein (1994), "Trustworthiness as a source of competitive advantage", *Strategic Management Journal*, 15:175–190.

Basel Committee on Banking Supervision (2005), *Basel II: Revised international capital framework*.

Beth, T. & M. Borcherding & B. Klein (1994), "Valuation of trust in open networks", in D. Gollman, ed., Computer Security --- *ESORICS '94* (Lecture Notes in Computer Science), pp. 3--18, Springer-Verlag Inc., New York, NY, USA.

Becker, L. C (1996), "Trust in Non-cognitive Security about Motives", *Ethics* 107 (October): 43-61.

Bikchandani, S. & D. Hirshleifer & I. Welch (1992), "A Theory of Fads, Fashion, Custom and Cultural Change as Informational Cascades", *J. Pol. Econ.,* 100(5) 992-1026.

Blaze, M. & J. Feigenbaum & J. Lacy (1996), "Decentralized Trust Management", *Proceedings of the IEEE Conference on Security and Privacy*, (Oakland, CA).

Blaze, M. & J. Feigenbaum & J. Ioannidis & A. Keromytis (1999), "The role of trust management in distributed systems security", *LNCS Secure Internet Programming*, vol. (1603), pp. 185-210. Springer-Verlag Inc., New York, NY, USA.

Bloom, D. E. (1998), "Technology Experimentation, and the Quality of Survey Data", *Science*, Vol. 280, no. 5365, pp 847-848.

Boston Consulting Group (1997), "Summary of Market Survey Results prepared for eTRUST", *The Boston Consulting Group*, San Francisco, CA.

Brands, S. (2000), "Rethinking Public Key Infrastructures and Digital Certificates", *MIT Press* (Cambridge, Massachusetts).

Burrows, M. & M. Abadi & R. M. Needham (1990), "A Logic of Authentication", *ACM Transactions on Computer Systems*, Vol. 8, No. 1, pp. 18-36.

Camenisch, J. & A. Lysyanskaya. An Efficient System for Non-transferable Anonymous Credentials with Optional Anonymity Revocation. In Advances in Cryptology -- EUROCRYPT 2001, B. Pfitzmann, Ed., 2001, Springer-Verlag LNCS 2045, pp. 93-118.

Camp, L. J. (2001), "An atomicity-generating layer for anonymous currencies", *IEEE Transactions on Software Engineering*, March, Vol. 27, No. 3, pp. 272-278.

Camp, L. J. & C. McGrath & H. Nissenbaum (2001), "Trust: A Collision of Paradigms", *LNCS Proceedings of Financial Cryptography*, Springer-Verlag Inc., New York, NY, USA.

Camp, L. J. & Carlos Osorio, (2003) "Privacy Enhancing Technologies for Internet Commerce," *Trust in the Network Economy*, eds. Otto Petrovic, Reinhard Posch, Franz Marhold. Springer-Verlag (Berlin) 2003. pp.317-329

Camp, L. J. & R. Tsang (2001), "Universal service in a ubiquitous digital network", *Journal of Ethics and Information Technology*, Vol. 2, No. 1. (Previously presented at INET 1999).

Camp, L. J. & C. Wolfram (2004), "Pricing Security", L. Jean Camp & Stephen Lewis, eds, *The Economics of Information Security*, Chapter 2, Vol. 12, Springer-Kluwer.

Caulkins (2001) "My reputation always had more fun than me", Richamond Journal of Law and Technology, Vol. 7, No. 4.

Cassell, J. & T. Bickmore (2000) "External Manifestations of Trustworthiness in the Interface", *Communications of the ACM*, December, Vol. 43 No. 12, pp 50-56.

Center for Democracy and Technology (2003) "Tracking Security at State Motor Vehicle Offices", http://www.cdt.org/privacy/030131motorvehicle.shtml project initiated April 14, 2003.

Chaum, D. (1985), "Security without Indentification: Transaction Systems to Make Big Brother Obsolete", *Communications of the ACM*, October, Vol. 28, No. 10.

Chaum, D. & A. Fiat & M. Naor (1988), "Untraceable Electronic Cash," *LNCS Advances in Cryptology CRYPTO '88*, S. Goldwasser (Ed.), Springer-Verlag, (Berlin, Germany).

Clark, D. & M. Blumenthal (2000), "Rethinking the design of the Internet: The end to end arguments vs. the brave new world", *Telecommunications Policy Research Conference*, Washington DC.

Coleman, J. (1990), *Foundations of Social Theory*, Belknap Press, Cambridge, MA.

Compaine, B. J. (1988), *Issues in New Information Technology*, Ablex Publishing, Norwood, NJ.

Computer Science and Telecommunications Board (1994), *Rights and Responsibilities of Participants in Networked Communities*, National Academy Press, Washington, D.C.

Computer Science and Telecommunications Board & National Research Council (2003), *Who Goes There?: Authentication Through the Lens of Privacy*, National Academy Press, Washington, DC.

Computer Science and Telecommunications Board & National Research Council (2001), *IDs – Not That Easy*, National Academy Press, Washington, DC.

Council for International Business (1993), *Statement of the United States Council for International Business on the Key Escrow Chip*, United States Council for International Business, NY, NY.

Cox, T. H. & S. A. Lobel & P. L. McLeod (1991), "Effects of Ethnic Group Cultural Differences on Cooperative and Competitive Behavior on a Group Task". *Academy of Management*, Vol. 34, No. 4, pp. 827-847.

Cranorm L.F. & J. Reagle (1998), "Designing a Social Protocol: Lessons Learned from the Platform for Privacy Preferences Project", In Jeffrey K. MacKie-Mason and David Waterman, eds., *Telephony, the Internet, and the Media.* Lawrence Erlbaum Associates.

Daugman, J. (2003), "The importance of being random: Statistical principles of iris recognition", *Pattern Recognition*, vol. 36, no. 2, pp. 279-291.

Davida, G. I. & Y. Frankel & B. J. Matt (1998), "On Enabling Secure Applications Through Off-Line Biometric Identification", *IEEE Symposium on Security and Privacy*. Oakland, CA.

Dawes, R.M & J. McTavish & H. Shaklee (1977) "Behavior, communication, and assumptions about other people's behavior in a commons dilemma situation", *Journal of Personality and Social Psychology*, Vol 35, pp 1-11.

Dellarocas, C. (2001), "Analyzing the Economic Efficiency of eBay-like Online Reputation Reporting Mechanisms", *Proc. 3rd ACM Conf. on Electronic Commerce*.

Dellarocas, C. (2002), "Efficiency and Robustness of Mediated Online Feedback Mechanisms: The Case of eBay", *SITE '02*.

Dingledine, R. & D. Molnar (2001), "Accountability", *Peer-to-peer: Harnessing the power technologies*, ch. 16, O'Reilly & Associates, (Cambridge, MA).

Dingledine, R. & N. Mathewson, & P. Syverson Tor: The Second-Generation Onion Router. In Proceedings of the 13th USENIX Security Symposium, August 2004, pp. 303-319.

Donath, J. & D. Boyd (2004), "Public displays of connection", *BT Technology Journal*, 22(4).

Dwork, C. & A. Goldberg & M. Naor (2003), "On Memory-Bound Functions for Fighting Spam", in D. Boneh (Ed.): *Advances in Cryptology-CRYPTO 2003, LNCS 2729*, Springer Verlag, pp. 426-444.

Dwork, C. & M. Naor (1992), "Pricing via Processing or Combating Junk Mail", in E. F. Brick (Ed.): *Advances in Cryptology-CRYPTO 1992, LNCS 740*, Springer Verlag, pp. 139-147.

Ellison, C. (2003), "Implications with Identity in PKI", ed. L. J. Camp, *Identity: The Digital Government Civic Scenario Workshop*, Boston, MA. http://www.ksg.harvard.edu/digitalcenter/conference/papers/pki.htm

Ericsson, K.A., & , H.A. Simon (1984), *Protocol analysis: Verbal reports as data.* Cambridge, MA: MIT Press.

Evensky, D. & A. Gentile & L. J. Camp & R. Armstrong (1997) "Lilith: Scalable Execution of User Code for Distributed Computing", *Proc. of The 6th IEEE International Symposium on High Performance Distributed Computing*, HPDC-6, Portland, OR, pp. 123-145.

Federal Trade Commission (2002) *ID Theft: When Bad Things Happen to Your Good Name.*

Federal Trade Commission, (2002) *Information on Identity Theft for Consumers and Victims from January 2002 Through December 2002*," http://www.consumer.gov/idtheft/reports/CY2002ReportFinal.pdf, date last viewed 11 April 2003.

Federal Trade Commission (2004), *FTC Releases Top 10 consumer Complaints for 2004*, Federal Trade Commission, http://www.ftc.gov/opa/2005/02/top102005.htm (last access 2/10/05).

Feldman, M. & K. Lai & I. Stoica & J. Chuang (2004), "Robust incentive techniques for peer-to-peer networks", *Proc. of EC '04*.

Friedman, B. ed. (2001), *Human Values and the Design of Computer Technology*, C S L I Publications.

Friedman, B. & L. Millett (2001), "Reasoning About Computers as Moral Agents", *Human Values and the Design of Computer Technology*, Batya Friedman (Editor), C S L I Publications.

Friedman, B. & P.H. Kahn Jr. D.C. Howe (2000) "Trust Online", *Com. of the ACM*, December , Vol. 43, No.12 34-40.

Friedman, E & P. Resnick (2001), "The Social Cost of Cheap Pseudonyms", *J. Economics and Management Strategy*, 10(2) 173-199.

Fernandes, A.D. (2001), "Risking trust in a public key infrastructure: old techniques of managing risk applied to new technology", *Decision Support Systems*, Vol. 31, pp. 303-322.

Foley, M. J. (2000), "Can Microsoft Squash 63,000 Bugs in Win2k?", *ZDnet Eweek, on-line edition*, 11 February 2000.

Foner, L. N. (1997), "Yenta: A Multi-Agent, Referral Based Matchmaking System", *First Int'l Conference on Autonomous Agents* (Agents '97), Marina del Rey, California.

Fukuyama, F. (1996), *Trust: The Social Virtues and the Creation of Prosperity*, Free Press, NY, NY.

Garfinkle, S. (1994), *PGP: Pretty Good Privacy*, O'Reilly & Associates, Inc., Sebastopol, CA, pp. 235-236.

Garfinkle, S. (2000), *Database Nation*, O'Reilly & Associates, Inc. (Sebastopol, CA).

Gefen, D. (2000), "E-commerce: the role of familiarity and trust", *Int'l Journal of Management Science*, 28:725–737.

General Accounting Office (2002), *Identity Theft: Greater Awareness and Use of Existing Data Are Needed*, GAO-02-776, Washington, DC.

Goldschlag, D. & M. Reed & P. Syverson (1999), "Onion Routing for Anonymous and Private Internet Connections", *Communications of the ACM*, v. 42, n. 2.

Herbert, Ian (2005) "No evidence against man in child porn inquiry who 'killed himself'", 1 October 2005, *The Independent*. available at: http://news.independent.co.uk/uk/legal/article316391.ece

Hochheiser, H. (2002), "The platform for privacy preference as a social protocol: An examination within the U.S. policy context", *ACM Trans. Inter. Tech.* 2, 4 (Nov. 2002), 276-306.

Hoffman, L. & Clark P (1991), "Imminent policy considerations in the design and management of national and international computer networks", *IEEE Communications Magazine*, February, 68-74.

Hottell, M. & D. Carter & M. Deniszczuk (2006), "Predictors of Home-Based Wireless Security", Fifth Workshop on the Economics of Information Security, University of Cambridge, England, June 26-28

Hsu, S. and D. Fears, (2007) "As Bush's ID Plan Was Delayed, Coalition Formed Against It", *Washington Post*, 25 February 25, 2007; Page A08

Jin, Ginger Zhe and Kato, Andrew, (2005) "Price, Quality and Reputation: Evidence from an Online Field Experiment*", RAND Journal of Economics*, Accepted. Available at SSRN: http://ssrn.com/abstract=917315

Kalakota, R. and A.B. Whinston (1997), *Electronic Commerce*. Addison Wesley,Boston, MA, 251-282.

Keisler, S. & L. Sproull & K. Waters (1996), "A Prisoners Dilemma Experiments on Cooperation with People and Human-Like Computers", *J. of Personality and Social Psych*, Vol. 70, pp 47-65.

Keize, G. (2004), "Do-it-yourself phishing kits lead to more scams", *Information Week*, August 2004.

Kephart, J.O. & D. Chess & S. R. White (1993) "Computer Networks as Biological Systems", *IEEE SPECTRUM* May 1993.

Kerr, N. L. & C. M. Kaufman-Gilliland (1994), "Communication, Commitment and cooperation in social dilemmas", *Journal of Personality and Social Psychology*, Vol. 66, pp 513-529

Kim, K. & B. Prabhakar (2000). "Initial trust, perceived risk, and the adoption of internet banking", *Proceedings of the Twenty First International Conference on Information Systems*.

Krackhardt, D. & J. Blythe & C. McGrath (1995), *KrackPlot 3.0: User's Manual*. Analytic Technologies, Columbia, SC.

Lessig, L. & P. Resnick (1999), "Zoning Speech on the Internet: A Legal and Technical Model", *Michigan Law Review* Vol. 98, No. 2: 395-431.

LoPucki, (2001) Human Identification Theory, 80 *Tex. L. Rev.* 114.

Luhmann, N. (1979) "Trust: A Mechanism For the Reduction of Social Complexity." *Trust and Power: Two works by Niklas Luhmann*. New York: John Wiley & Sons, pp. 1-103.

Lyon, D. (2001), *Surveillance Society – Monitoring Everyday Life*, Open University Press: Buckinghamshire, 2001.

Mansfield, T. & J. L. Wayman (2000) *Best Practices in Testing and Reporting Performance of Biometric Devices*, Version 1.0, http://www.afb.org.uk/bwg/bestprac10.pdf

Meadows, C.A. (1995) "Formal Verification of Cryptographic Protocols: A Survey", *Proc. of ASIACRYPT: Advances in Cryptology -- ASIACRYPT: Int'l Conference on the Theory and Application of Cryptology*, IEEE Computer Society Press, Washington DC.

Mulligan, Deirdre and Jerry Berman, (1999) "Privacy in the Digital Age: Work in Progress," *Nova Law Review*, Volume 23, Number 2, Winter 1999.

McAdams, R. H (1995) "Cooperation and conflict: The economics of group status production and race discrimination", *Harvard Law Review*, Vol. 108, No. 5, pp. 1003-1084, March.

Microsoft Research (2006a) *Biometric ID: Technical Overview*, available http://download.microsoft.com/download/d/6/b/d6bde980-5568-4926-8c71-dea63befed64/biometric_id.doc. Last viewed 12/06.

Microsoft Research (2006b) Microsoft Tamper resistant Biometric ID Cards, available at http://research.microsoft.com/msbit/Factsheet.doc, Last viewed 12/06.

National Research Council (1996), *Cryptography's Role in Securing the Information Society*, Nat'l Academy Press, (Wash, DC.)

Newell, A. & H. A. Simon (1972), *Human problem solving*, Englewood Cliffs, NJ: Prentice-Hall.

Newton, E. M. & J. D. Woodward (2001) "Biometrics: A Technical Primer," John D. Woodward, Katherine W. Webb, Elaine M. Newton et al., Appendix A, "Biometrics: A Technical Primer," "Army Biometric Applications: Identifying and Addressing Sociocultural Concerns," RAND/MR-1237-A, Santa Monica, CA.

Nikander, P. & K. Karvonen (2001), "Users and Trust in Cyberspace", *Security Protocols - 9th International Workshop, Springer LNCS*, Verlag (Berlin, Germany).

Nissenbaum, H. (2001), "Securing Trust Online: Wisdom or Oxymoron", *Boston University Law Review* June. Volume 81, No.3 635-664

Nissenbaum, H. & E. Felton & B. Friedman (2002), "Computer Security: Competing Concepts", *30th Research Conference on Communication, Information and Internet Policy*, Washington D.C.

Miller, N. & P. Resnick & R. Zeckhauser (2002), "Eliciting Honest Feedback in Electronic Markets", *SITE '02*.

O'Harrow, Robert Jr., (2001) "Concerns for ID Theft Often Are Unheeded", *Washington Post*, July 23, 2001; Page A01.

Office of Technology Assessment (1985), *Electronic Surveillance and Civil Liberties OTA-CIT-293*, United States Government Printing Office; Gaithersburg, MA.

Office of Technology Assessment (1986), *Management, Security and Congressional Oversight OTA-CIT-297*, United States Government Printing Office; Gaithersburg, MA.

Pear, Robert, (2007) "Warnings over Privacy of US Health Network", *New York Times*, 16A, columns 3-5, 18 February.

Perlman, R. (1999), "An overview of PKI trust models", *IEEE Network*, Vol. 13, pp. 38-43, Nov/Dec.

Pew Internet and American Life Project (2005), *Trust and privacy online: Why Americans want to rewrite the rules.* PEW Internet & American Life Project, NY, NY

Pew Internet and American Life Project (2002a) *On-line rating Systems*, PEW Internet & American Life Project, NY, NY, February 2002.

Pew Internet and American Life Project (2002b) *What consumers have to say about information privacy*, PEW Internet & American Life Project, NY, NY, February 2002.

Phillips, P. J. & A. Martin & C. L. Wilson & M. Przybocki (2000), "An Introduction to Evaluating Biometric Systems", *IEEE Computer*, February 2000, pp. 56-63.

Phillips, P.J. & H. Moon & S. Rizvi & P. Rauss (2000), "The FERET Evaluation methodology for face-recognition algorithms", *IEEE trans. PAMI*, Vol. 22, No. 10.

Pierce, Deborah, (2003) "Opinion: Swiping driver's licenses—instant marketing lists?," *Seattle Press*, March 31, 2003.

Paoulson, K. (2006) "MySpace Predator Caught By Code", *Wired News,* 6 Oct 2006, http://www.wired.com/news/technology/1,71948-0.html.

Rangan, P. V. (1988) "An Axiomatic Basis for Trust in Distributed Systems ", *Proc. of the 1988 IEEE Sym. on Security and Privacy*, pp. 204-211, IEEE Computer Society Press, Washington DC.

Raul, A.C. (2002), *Privacy and the Digital State: Balancing Public Information and Personal Privacy.* Kluwer: Norwell, MA.

Regan, P. (1995), "Legislating Privacy: Technology, Social Values and Public Policy", *Business Ethics Quarterly* 8 (4), p. 723-724.

Resnick, P. & R. Zeckhauser & E. Friedman & K. Kuwabara (2000) "Reputation Systems", *CACM*, Vol. 43, No. 12, Dec. 45-48.

Rubin, L. & R. Cooter (1994), *The Payment System: Cases Materials and Issues*, West Publishing Co.; St. Paul, MN.

Schneider, F. (ed) (1999), *Trust in Cyberspace*, National Academies Press, Washington D.C.

Schneier, B. (2002), "Computer Security: It's the Economics, Stupid", *Workshop Econ, and Information Security*, Berkeley, CA.

Schneier, B. (1995), *Applied Cryptography, Second Edition*, John Wiley & Sons, Inc., New York, NY.

Schneiderman, B. (2000), "Designing Trust into Online Experiences", *CACM*, December, Vol. 43 No. 12, pp57-59.

Schwartz, A. (2002), "Driver's License Security", *Testimony Before the House Committee on Transportation and Infrastructure* Subcommittee on Highways and Transit, September 5, 2002.

Schwartz, Ari (2000) "HR 4049 Privacy Commission Act", *Testimony Before The House Committee on Government Reform* Subcommittee On Government Management, Information and Technology, April 12, 2000.

Shostack, Adam, (2002) "Privacy Invasion Infrastructure Subsidies," *CACR*, Toronto (CN) March 13, 2002.

Sullivan, Bob, (2003) "ID Theft Costs Banks $1 Billion A Year," http://www.msnbc.com/news/891186.asp Last Visited: April 15, 2003

Seamons, K. E. & M. Winslett & T. Yu & L. Yu & R. Jarvis, "Protecting Privacy During On-line Trust Negotiation", *Privacy Enhancing Technologies 2002*, R. Dingledine and P. Syverson (Eds.), Springer-Verlag, LNCS 2482, (Berlin, Germany).

Seligman, A. (1997), *The Problem of Trust*. Princeton University Press (Princeton, NJ)

Shostack, A. (2003), "Paying for Privacy: Consumers and Infrastructures", *Wrksp on Econ and Info, Sec.,* College Park, MD.

Slovic, P. (1993), "Perceived Risk, Trust, and Democracy", *Risk Analysis* Vol. 13, No. 6 675-681.

Smith, Greg (2007) "Teacher Guilty in Norwood Porn Case", Norwich Bulletin, Saturday January 6, available at: http://www.norwichbulletin.com/apps/pbcs.dll/article?AID=/20070106/NEWS01/701060312/1002/NEWS17

Sophos (2002), "Melissa was 'a colossal mistake' says author", Sophos Prsss Release, http://www.sophos.com/virusinfo/articles/melissa2.html

Sproull, L. & S. Kiesler (1991), *Connections*, The MIT Press, Cambridge, MA.

Stubblebine, S. G. & P. F. Syverson (2000), "Authentic Attributes with Fine-Grained Anonymity Protection", *Financial Cryptography (FC 2000)*, Y. Frankel (Ed.), Springer-Verlag, LNCS 1962, Berlin, Germany.

Su, J. & J. D. Tygar (1996), "Building blocks for atomicity in electronic commerce", *Proc. of USENIX Security Symposium*, USENIX Association, Berkeley, CA.

Sullivan, B. (2003) "The darkest side of ID theft", MSNBC.com, <http://www.msnbc.com/news/877978.asp?0si=-&cp1=1>.

Syverson, P. F. (2003), "The Paradoxical Value of Privacy", *Workshop on Economics and Info Security*, College Park, MD.

Tang, L. (1996), "Verifiable Transaction Atomicity for Electronic Payment Systems", *Proc. of the 16th Int'l Conf. on Distributed Computing Systems*. IEEE Computer Society Press.

Taylor, N. (2002) "State Surveillance and the Right to Privacy". *Surveillance & Society*, (1) 66-85.

Tygar, J. D. & A. Whitten, (1996), "WWW Electronic Commerce and Java Trojan Horses", *Proc. of the Second USENIX Workshop on Electronic Commerce*, 18-21 Oakland, CA, pp 243-249

Tyler, T. R. (1990), "Justice, Self-Interest, and the legitimacy of Legal and Political Authority". *Beyond Self-Interest*, ed. J. J. Mansbridge. Chicago and London: The University of Chicago Press.

Tyler, T. (1990), *Why People Obey the Law,* Yale University Press (New Haven, CT).

USA PATRIOT Act (2001) [Section 326, among others].

United States Senate Committee on Governmental Affairs Subcommittee on Oversight of Government Management (2002), Restructuring, and the District of Columbia, *Hearing: A License to Break the Law? Protecting the Integrity of Driver's Licenses*, April 16, 2002 (Witness List: http://www.senate.gov/~gov_affairs/041602witness.htm)

Van den Hoven, J. (1997), "Privacy and the Varieties of Informational Wrongdoing", in Spinello & Tavani (eds) *Readings in Cyberethics*, Jones & Bartlett: Sudbury, p. 430-442.

Varian, H. (2002), "System Reliability and Free Riding", *Economics and Information Security Workshop*, Berkeley, CA.

Viega, J. & Y. Kohno & B. Potter (2001) "Trust (and mistrust) in secure applications", *CACM*, February, Vol 44, No. 2, pp36.

Yahalom, R. & B. Klein B. & T. Beth (1993), "Trust relationships in secure systems---A distributed authentication perspective", *Proc. of the IEEE Symposium on Research in Security and Privacy*, pp. 150--164.

Wacker, J. (1995), "Drafting agreements for secure electronic commerce", *Proc. of the World Wide Electronic Commerce: Law, Policy, Security & Controls Conference*, Washington, DC, pp. 6.

Walden, I. (1995), "Are privacy requirements inhibiting electronic commerce," *Proc. of the World Wide Electronic Commerce: Law, Policy, Security & Controls Conference*, Washington, DC, pp. 10.

Y Wang, D Berck, Z Jiang, et. al., (2006) "Automated Web Partol with Strider Honey Mondekeys", *Proc. of Network and Distributed System Security*, ISOC Publishing (Washington DC).   Weick, K.E. (1990), "Technology as equivoque: Sense-making in new technologies", P.S. Goodman, L.S. Sproull (eds.), *Technology and Organizations* (pp. 1-44). San Francisco, CA: Jossey-Bass.

Weisband, S. & S. Kiesler (1996), "Self Disclosure on computer forms: Meta-analysis and implications", *Proc. of the CHI '96 Conference on Human-Computer Interaction*, Vancouver, BC, Canada.

Whitten, A. and J.D. Tygar (1999), "Why Johnny Can't Encrypt: A Usability Evaluation of PGP 5.0", *Proceedings of the 8th USENIX Security Symposium*, USENIX Association, Berkeley, CA.

Williams, M (2001), "In whom we trust: Group membership as an affective context for trust development", *Academy of Management Review*, Vol. 26, No. 3, pp-377-396.

Winslett, M. & T. Yu & K. E. Seamons & A. Hess & J. Jacobson & R. Jarvis & B. Smith & L. Yu (2002), "Negotiating Trust on the Web", *IEEE Internet Computing*, November/December 2002.

Wit, A.P. & H. A. M. Wilke (1992), "The Effect of Social Categorization on Cooperation in Three Types of Social Dilemmas", *Journal of Economic Psychology*, v13n1, 135-151, March, 17 pp.

Yee, B. & R. Blackley (2003) "Trusting Code and Trusting Hardware", edited by L. J. Camp, *Identity: The Digital Government Civic Scenario Worksho*p, Boston, MA. http://www.ksg.harvard.edu/digitalcenter/conference/papers/codeanHW.htm

Zwicky, E. D. & S. Cooper & D. B. Chapman (2000*), Building Internet Firewalls*, Second Edition. O'Reilly and Associates, Sebastopol, California.

20. Index

R

RealID, xi, 43, 45, 46, 47, 166
robust, 16, 110, 111, 121, 123, 149, 152, 154
robustness, 110, 119, 122

S

signal, 4, 56, 57, 58, 78
Social Security Number, 7, 8, 12, 17, 18, 21, 22, 24, 31, 49, 64, 93, 139, 169, 170

SSN, 2, 7, 9, 17, 18, 21, 22, 50, 168
spam, 34, 51, 56, 74, 76, 78, 97, 98, 99, 108

T

tokens, 15, 96, 97, 115

V

Verification, 40, 47, 48, 110, 111, 115, 119, 120, 123, 178

Printed in the United States of America.